Bad Girls and Other Perils

BAD GIRLS

and other perils

MIKE STROBEL

DUNDURN PRESS

TORONTO

Editor: Nicole Chaplin
Design: Courtney Horner
Printer: Transcontinental

Library and Archives Canada Cataloguing in Publication

Strobel, Mike
        Bad girls and other perils / by Mike Strobel.

Also issued in electronic format.
ISBN 978-1-55488-786-6

        I. Title.

AC8.S77 2010   081   C2010-902442-7

1   2   3   4   5   14   13   12   11   10

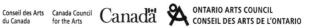

We acknowledge the support of the **Canada Council for the Arts** and the **Ontario Arts Council** for our publishing program. We also acknowledge the financial support of the **Government of Canada** through the **Canada Book Fund** and **The Association for the Export of Canadian Books**, and the **Government of Ontario** through the **Ontario Book Publishers Tax Credit program**, and the **Ontario Media Development Corporation**.

J. Kirk Howard, President

www.dundurn.com

Dundurn Press
3 Church Street, Suite 500
Toronto, Ontario, Canada
M5E 1M2

Gazelle Book Services Limited
White Cross Mills
High Town, Lancaster, England
LA1 4XS

Dundurn Press
2250 Military Road
Tonawanda, NY
U.S.A. 14150

For Jackson: my son, my muse, my star.

CONTENTS

PREFACE

Catchy title, eh? No matter how you say it. *Bad* Girls. Bad *Girls*. I know, it's tacky. But I've been in the newspaper game for 30 years, much of it with the saucy *Toronto Sun*, and I know damn well what sells. Bad girls sell.

Now that you've bought the book, though, I hope you read it all, not just the chapter on women gone wrong. Boys go wrong, too, you know. So do politicians, bureaucrats, entertainers, athletes, businessmen, kids, beauty queens, doctors, swingers, nudists ... and, of course, fans of the Montreal

Canadiens. They're all in this book, as are many others.

It is part of a columnist's job to point out when people, animals, or even plants go bad. This duty leaves most of us bitter, negative, and drained of empathy. While some folks, especially PR agents, suck up to us, most fear and loathe us. We have few friends except for other columnists.

There's an old saw that reporters and photographers wage the real battles and columnists are the ones who, when the fighting is over, emerge from the woods to shoot the wounded. That's an ugly image to live up to, but we try.

Public figures sure make it easy for us.

Of course, we would become too twisted to be of any use if all we did was finish off the casualties of life. There are few tasks more satisfying than righting wrongs or instigating change and in this job you get to do both. Once in a while.

If you write the kind of columns I write, you also get to schmooze with the beautiful, poke fun at the famous, play sportswriter, mingle with the world's weirdest people, dispense advice on all manner of critical human functions, and share time with real heroes.

Is there a better job in the world? If you have one, you are indeed blessed.

In fact, I gave up a pretty good gig to go columnizing. Being editor-in-chief of a paper like the *Sun* has its perks, but it also involves suits, piles of paperwork, and endless meetings.

Not to mention dealing with high-strung, egomaniacal columnists.

But what's even more valuable are the people you work with, and that's especially true at a tight ship like the *Sun*. A few names come quickly to mind: The genius wit Andy Donato, who drew the cover. Also, Doug, Lester, Gordie, Lou, Jamie, the Baron, Bono, Sully, Durkan, Worthington, Mare, Poole, Kev, The *Sun City*, news and photo desks, Linda, Parker, MBG, JK, PVG, Big Mark, Scrawler, Lorrie, and Nicole at Dundurn ... but I'll stop there: there are thousands to thank and book paper is expensive.

Julie Kirsh inspired this volume and it would not have come to pass without her and her research staff. Columnists who publish collections always thank their readers, even the ones who write to call them names or threaten to break their nose. So shall I.

I hope you enjoy the book. Even if you're only interested in bad girls.

IN THE LADIES ROOM

Her? Poor? That's Rich!
(March 8, 2002)

Down the alley we scurry. The Shaky Lady is moving like a cat now, her little pull-cart bouncing behind her.

She glances back, spots me as I duck behind a garbage bin in the gloom. For a second our eyes lock. Hers are clear and wary.

Her two bodyguards. Where are they? She darts round a

The Shaky Lady at work on her favourite downtown corner.

corner. I hear a car door slam.

Now I'm running, panting. *Gawd*, I think, *I can't keep up with a bag lady.*

She's at least 65.

I lurch around the corner. Into the glare of headlights ...

— — —

Hours earlier, Yonge and Bloor:

Man, the Shaky Lady is a pitiful sight. She sits on the northwest corner. Her head and hands shake grotesquely, constantly. She wears a shabby red jacket. Her hair is grey and scraggly under a faded purple kerchief.

A garbage bag covers her legs. People throw money on it. Lots of people. Sometimes they line up.

"She got here about 11," says Const. Paul Stone, 50, on traffic duty at a construction site. "She started shaking as soon as she sat down. She's just raking it in now."

In our spy nest at Harvey's across the street, photographer Alex Urosevic and I do some figuring.

Thirty people in 15 minutes, Alex counts. Fifty in the time it takes me to eat a veggie burger and sip a coffee. So, be very conservative and say 50 kind strangers an hour, a toonie each, five hours a day, five days a week.

That's $2,500 a week. Net. I mean, what's the overhead? How much do blue thermal pants and a garbage bag cost?

Above the Shaky Lady's roost rises a CIBC tower. How many of those bankers take home that kind of dough?

I wander over to get a closer look. Several people in the area have told me she usually has two burly men keeping watch over her. Some think they're her sons.

If they're around, I can't spot them in the throngs.

"Please help me. I'm sick and poor. I will pray for you," says the cardboard sign around her neck.

I toss in a toonie. She gives me a toothless grin and croaks. The shaking is remarkable. How could you say no?

Shopkeepers and security staff say she has haunted Bloor between Yonge and Bay for at least a year.

"I was struck by her wretched appearance," says Agnes McKenna, 74, who lives nearby. "I wondered, how could anybody be so heartless as to dump her on the street?

"A couple of weeks ago, coming home from a meeting, I see this woman suddenly get up, spry as a chicken. Her face becomes alive, she packs up her buggy and off she goes. Makes you feel like a fool, to be taken like that."

Toronto Police Constable Andrew Hassall once saw a woman so torn up about the Shaky Lady she bought her a $200 coat at The Bay. The beggar croaked her thanks, waited for the woman to leave, then threw out the coat. Hassall couldn't persuade the kind woman she'd been had.

The Shaky Lady is "the prima donna of this sort of thing," says Hassall. "She's been a thorn in our sides for years."

But the cops are stuck. Panhandling is legal.

Down Bloor, I catch up to two of her benefactors. Judy Gerich, 53, an Edmonton teacher and sister Debbie Galloway, 46, a daycare operator, gave the Shaky Lady $30. Then they brought her coffee and chicken fingers.

"I couldn't believe how she looked," says Debbie. "It rips your heart out."

For a while, I hide by the construction site behind the Shaky Lady. They are laying fibre-optic cable.

I can see each person approach the woman. I see horror, pity. I see $10 bills, a few twenties. She tucks them under the bag. I think our income estimate is low.

At 4:30 p.m. she gets up, chucks the sisters' chicken fingers in the garbage and heads west on Bloor. There is no shaking. She moves faster and faster.

Into the alley ...

... I round the corner. A car, a Chevy Lumina, speeds in reverse. A man drives, another sits in the back. The Shaky Lady, kerchief off, crouches in the passenger seat.

Caught without cover, I give chase. I can't read the plate. Alex is in an alley away, trying to cut them off.

But the Lumina pulls out on Balmuto Street, by the Uptown Theatre, then west on Bloor.

By the time I hail a cab and yell "Follow that Lumina!" it's gone. Who knows where?

But I'm guessing it's not to a shelter for the homeless.

Mom Warned You About Them
(May 29, 2008)

Men, as women know, often store their brains just south of their belt buckle. This leads to fuzzy logic and dangerous liaisons, especially for males in positions of power.

It's too late to help ex-foreign affairs minister Maxime Bernier. But now seems a good time for a manual on how to spot and avoid a *Femme Fatale* (FF).

First, fellas, let's review. What exactly is a femme fatale?

My Canadian Oxford says: "A woman to whom a person feels irresistibly attracted, usually with dangerous or unhappy results."

History teems with examples. Adam had Eve. Samson, Delilah. Marc Antony, Cleopatra. The Renaissance had Lucrezia Borgia. The First World War had Mata Hari.

Film FFs are legion. Garbo. Dietrich. Rita Hayworth. Catwoman. Desperate Housewives. Paula Abdul.

There are hommes fatals, too, of course. Bad Boys.

James Bond, Dracula, Colin Farrell, Brando, P. Diddy, and Pierre Trudeau come to mind. But Adam's rib is the rub. Or the flub, in Bernier's case.

Now, how to recognize a femme fatale.

Well, if the lady is blond, you are probably safe, though exceptions include the Sharon Stones and Marilyn Monroes of the world. Blondes are risky, sure, but in a good way.

You rarely get fired or die, hence no "fatale," though blondes can make you broke.

Same for redheads. Potentially lethal, but not devious like FFs. For instance, Red Sonja, She-Devil with a Sword, would as soon gut you as look at you.

A femme fatale is subtler. And usually dark-haired. So beware of brunettes and raven-tops.

(Sheesh, Strobe, can you narrow it down?)

A good rule of thumb: The darker the hair the deadlier the dame. Makes her mysterious, a key trait of FFs.

I mean, how many really mysterious blondes do you know?

Look at Cate Blanchett. Blonde, she's a virgin queen, a reporter, an elf. Dye her hair black and she's a Soviet agent battling Indiana Jones. Voila, femme fatale.

Head for the hills if she tries to get you drunk. A traditional FF ploy, this weakens your defences against her charms.

Still there, lad, like a sloppy puppy?

Well, flee if the drink tastes funny. Poison is another FF tradition, notably for Lucrezia. By no means is this the only tactic.

A classic FF and James Bond's adversary in GoldenEye, Xenia Onatopp, crushed men with her powerful thighs. Xenia had another common FF trait. An accent.

Again, this adds to their mystery, intrigue, and exotic nature. They say things like, "Comm vis me, dahling."

You will note Monsieur Bernier's femme fatale, Julie Couillard, has a French accent, though, come to think of it, so does Maxime.

Heels. The higher, the badder. So as to grind you into the ground like a bug.

She smokes. This clue is out of fashion, not to mention illegal in Toronto, as is the classic femme fatale cigarette holder. But if she chews Nicorette gum, slowly and sensually, run away.

She is quiet. Chatty Cathies are rarely femmes fatales. FFs draw you in with a glance, a wink, a licked lip. Loud jokes and "Hey, did you watch *Lost*?" are for Girls Next Door and their ilk.

If she beats you at pool, she's surefire trouble.

No Girl Next Door, Damsel in Distress, or Madonna Figure plays pool with skill. Tomboys do, but they snooker you in jeans. FFs beat you in silk, perfume and cleavage.

You mention NATO, and she doesn't ask, "Oh, do you mean NATO NY or NATO Miami?"

Femmes fatales don't flaunt it, but they know the GNP of Peru, who the president of Iceland is, and often have several languages.

But just one tattoo. Your lady has several? They're garish and combined with piercings? What you have, buster, is a rocker chick.

A femme fatale's tattoo is always hidden in a quiet place. So by the time you spot it, it's too late.

If it says "My Heart Belongs to Harley-Davidson," you are certainly sunk.

So, there you go. The Maxime Bernier Memorial Femme Fatale Manual.

Use at your own risk. Studies show for every femme fatale, there is un homme stupide.

Lust in Space
(February 7, 2007)

"Wow! Jeez!"
— Walter Cronkite, as the Eagle landed on the moon

Wow! Jeez! is right. Break out the heat tiles. This is hotter than the "Trouble With Tribbles" episode on the old *Star Trek*.

Unless you have been dead or on Mars, you know the story of a cosmic love triangle. Astronaut Lisa Nowak, who flew on the shuttle Discovery last July, is accused of Macing and trying to kidnap her romance rival, U.S. Air Force Captain Colleen Shipman. Nowak, 43, suspects Shipman of making stardust with spaceman Bill Oefelein, 41.

While hunting her foe, Nowak even wore diapers, as

astronauts do. So she could pee without needing to slip the surly bonds of her car.

John Glenn must have peed his pants when he heard.

Love triangle? Stalking? Shabby mug shots? This is not how astronauts act.

Jumpin' Jupiter. What happened?

I call my favourite shrink, Dr. Irvin Wolkoff, 54. He always has down-to-earth advice.

"She 'snapped,'" he tells me. "You have to wonder with all the wonderfulness of The Right Stuff, if a part of it isn't being a little bent.

"Some of the things that make a person valuable to be strapped on the end of a rocket don't bode well in relationships. She needs help. She has my sympathy. She was literally and figuratively as high as you can go in American culture."

Now, she wears a satellite tracking device.

And NASA yearns for the days of Tranquility.

Science author Laura Woodmansee, 35, is as shocked as anyone. Her *Women Astronauts* (Apogee Books) includes a bio on our Captain Nowak.

For instance, she flies 30 kinds of aircraft and once was assigned to the Electronic Warfare Aggressor Squadron. Yikes. I bet she was rated A in pepper spray.

"Nothing like this has ever happened before," Woodmansee tells me from California. "Or if it has, we haven't heard about it. And certainly not to this degree.

"It doesn't make sense, unless the pressure just got to her and she flipped out."

Astronauts work up to 20 hours a day. A misstep can cost them a mission or a career.

Not to mention, there's a chance they'll die in a fireball.

What draws them? A need for speed, partly. That shared addiction can lead to other kinds of sparks.

Nowak, who is married, and Oefelein, who is not, never

flew together. At least not in an aircraft.

What if they had?

Which leads us to Woodmansee's other book, *Sex in Space*.

So, it's true, Laura. There is a Zero G-spot.

"No one's admitting it, but the evidence is there," she says.

Newlyweds Jan Davis and Mark Lee flew on Endeavour in 1992. It is said crewmates allowed them honeymoon breaks in the — wink, wink — payload bay.

Aboard the space station Mir, two cosmonauts were caught flirting on video and, later, having a huge fight and not speaking for three weeks.

If that doesn't spell sex, I don't know what does.

But so far the only admitted orbital boinking has been by rats or Japanese Medaka fish.

Too bad. How many of you have sex so good you're bouncing off the ceiling?

Like it sweaty? Well, sweat doesn't evaporate in space.

Mile-high club? Amateurs.

"People make sex in space sound like it would be really difficult, with bungee cords and Velcro," says Woodmansee. "If you just hang on to each other, you'll be fine."

Not that astronaut Nowak will ever get that chance, though she and Oefelein were up for more missions.

NASA frowns on misuse of diapers. And attempted murder.

Not even Wernher von Braun could get this career back off the ground.

Hard to see an upside in this tale of Lust in Space.

"Well, it shows astronauts are human," says Woodmansee.

They can be as horny, as wacky, as flawed as the rest of us. We are shocked because they have long seemed as shiny and perfect as the stars they seek.

The higher they are, the farther they fall.

You can't help feeling sorry for her.

Godspeed Lisa Nowak.

Who You Calling a Witch?
(January 27, 2008)

Miss Canada Plus is on the phone. The lovely Stephanie Conover, 23, of East York.

I was a judge in the pageant that picked her last fall. She has 10 tattoos, but she's a sweetheart.

Now, she's really steamed.

"This is outraaaaaageous," she says.

Careful, Stephanie, your belly button ring will pop. What's up?

So she tells me how she got an invite three weeks ago to be a judge at the Miss Toronto Tourism pageant.

She was thrilled. She has been a busy Miss Canada Plus, including charities from women's shelters to food banks to multiple sclerosis. But this was her first gig as a pageant judge.

And Miss Toronto Tourism has high ideals, promoting our city's attractions, multiculturalism, and generosity.

Stephanie settled on an empress green gown, strapless with a to-die-for bodice, and eagerly awaited the February 2 gala.

They asked for a bio for the program and she included her hobbies: songwriting, dancing, painting, knitting, making custom jewelry, yoga, reiki (a Japanese healing art), and tarot cards.

This week, her Miss Canada Plus handlers got a letter back:

"Upon receiving her bio," it said, "we have decided against her being a judge. We need a judge who has an upright reputation, (who) we would be proud to introduce to the audience."

Holy smokes. What does the Miss Toronto Tourism pageant have against knitting? Or dancing? Miss Canada Plus can shake a leg, but it does not involve a pole.

The dismissal letter continues:

"She states that her hobbies are yoga, reiki and tarot card reading. Our board of directors has eliminated her as a judge as tarot card reading and reiki are the occult and ... not acceptable by God, Jews, Muslims or Christians."

Then there's a Biblical quote about mediums and "spiritists."

Then: "We hope that Stephanie Conover will turn from these belief systems and will repent from her practice of them."

I trot down to Totum Life Science, the King Street West gym where Stephanie works, to see if she wants to repent.

She does not.

Her honey-brown eyes snap and crackle.

"Completely preposterous," she says. "My mother is an Anglican and she's furious, too. My first thought was, this is quite something for the City to be telling me."

Actually, Miss Toronto Tourism is independent, having nil to do with City Hall or with the tourism board, say spokesmen for both.

"But charities benefit and that's the important thing," one tells me.

The pageant has garnered regular press since it debuted in 1999, not all of it good.

Zenovique Wilson, 20, was on bail for robbery of a massage parlour when she won the 2005 crown. Charges were later stayed.

Current entry rules include "no criminal offences," "good will to others," and "born female."

The likes of yoga, reiki, and tarot are taboo, too, apparently, at least for judges.

"We are not a religious pageant," director Karyn Murray assures me. She says folks of many backgrounds will be at the waterfront Radisson Admiral hotel on the big night. "We don't want to offend anybody."

She tells me there were also fears Stephanie would use tarot cards to choose a winner.

"That's silly," snorts Stephanie.

No kidding. I've judged many pageants. Usually, I go "eeny, meeny, miny, moe."

Ms Murray tells me her judges include a service club executive and a magazine publisher.

The emcee is Elvis impersonator Dorian Baxter, better known as Elvis Priestly.

There will be jazz and salsa dancers.

If the Miss Toronto Tourism brass doesn't like Stephanie Conover's hobbies, wait'll they hear this: she sings in a (shudder) hip hop band.

Oh, and she's a Wiccan.

Yep, she tells me, she's a witch. A WITCH!

A good witch. "I don't commune with dark forces."

Thus no need to hang garlic in the pageant ballroom.

"We don't even believe in the devil," says Stephanie. "We believe whatever you send out into the world, good or bad, comes back to you, times three."

So there you have it.

A pageant boasting many colours and creeds, Latin entertainment, an Elvis impersonator as a host, and a witch as a defrocked judge.

My goodness. This really is a multicultural town.

Well, He Sure Got to Third Base
(September 21, 2005)

I happened to be at the beer stand when Jose Canseco cracked that dilly to left field in the 1989 American League championship series.

But I sure heard it. That awful whack, the whoosh of the crowd. First homer to rattle the upper deck at SkyDome.

So we knew Jose Canseco swung a mighty bat.

Now we know he had itsy-bitsy balls.

Now we know (hang on to your peanuts) his Louisville Slugger was, well, uncut.

Now we know he never went nine innings, that he loved to watch himself pitching woo in the mirror.

Now we know he showered only every two, three days.

My gawd, fellas, be good to your missus. She might write a book about you.

Meet Jessica Canseco, 31, ex of Jose. We are in SkyBox 2 at what is now called the Rogers Centre.

I am surprised to find she is blonde and gorgeous. She's in torn True Religion jeans and Roberto Cavalli blouse.

Just to starboard is Section 540, Row 5, Seat 6, where that ALCS dinger landed in the hand of a classical singer named Jake Neely. Canseco's A's went on to win the World Series.

That was before Jessica Sekely met Jose.

At that point, she was Sweet 16 and her only brush with greatness, so to speak, was Metallica drummer Lars Ulrich. She almost gave him oral sex backstage.

Almost? Well, read the book. *Juicy: Confessions of a Former Baseball Wife.*

It's a hoot.

Here is Jessica's plot: she gets a boob job, works at Hooters in Cleveland. Jose Canseco comes in.

Ooooh, is he ever gorgeous. He buys her $4,000 worth of neat clothes.

She's hooked. She sleeps with him in Boston.

"It didn't look like any wiener I'd ever seen before." Two years later, she has an orgasm.

She learns to shoot steroids in his buttocks. The drugs shrink his testicles. He runs around with groupies. Lots of them. Every port in the big leagues.

Still, they do it on the bathroom floor, the dining room table, the cave behind their waterfall, the Porsche. (Who hasn't?)

They also have a cougar and a lynx. Real ones, not cars. Plus an iguana and miniature schnauzers. Wink, wink.

But they don't talk.

Well, sometimes.

Jose: "You took drugs!"

Jessica: "Oh, big deal. I took a little Ecstasy!"

Jose: "I had it analyzed at the lab. It was speed!"

Jessica *(to herself)*: "So that's why I was up all night cleaning!"

Mostly, Jose is a "horrible, lying cheat."

She leaves. She's pregnant. She stays. She shops. They wed. She leaves. No, wait, she stays. She files for divorce. She comes back. He files for divorce.

She leaves. They divorce. She stays, anyway. She leaves. (Quick, bring in the closer.) Her father, turns out, was a transvestite.

Oh, no. Must have been a shock to see Jose, 41, wearing lingerie on *The Surreal Life*.

"No. Jose is all about controversy."

No guff. His book *Juiced* helped rip open the MLB steroids scandal. Made Rafael Palmeiro a "horrible, lying cheat" too.

What does Jose think of your *Juicy*?

"He suggested I write it. He thought it would be more about steroids and players." (It's not, though she did sleep with a tight end, Kansas City Chief Tony Gonzalez.)

"At first Jose was sad. And he was angry about the acknowledgements." They include her new beau.

But Jose was okay with all that personal stuff?

"It was hard for him. Men don't want to hear they're insensitive or not good lovers.

"Would you want your ex-wife to write a book about you?"

Not if there's pictures, no. Especially not in bookstores everywhere.

But they both know what sells.

And there's an unwritten postscript: Jessica and Jose shacked up again for a while last year.

After all that stuff in the book?!

"It was for financial reasons, for our child (Jessie, 8), for me, whatever, we decided to see if we could try ... I knew it kind of wasn't going to work."

Sounds familiar.

"Sure, bring out the violins. But it's over now. It took the book and *Playboy* contracts to move my life forward."

She is September's cover.

Jose left her a message last weekend.

Misses her. "You're shadows of the girl I knew. I love you."

Too late, it's truly over, she tells me.

Besides, a groupie is living in his basement.

I smell a reality show in here somewhere.

Angelina, Jennifer: Enough of this Meow-Fest
(December 18, 2008)

If the recession is as long, bitter, and silly as the Angelina Jolie-Jennifer Aniston catfight, well, we're screwed.

Please. Someone lock those two ditzy dames in a cage, give them switchblades and get it over with. Sell tickets, proceeds to Variety Village.

Call it Angennifer Mania III.

I hoped the feline fur had finally stopped flying, until my checkout magazine rack started to sizzle again the past couple of weeks.

The cover of *US Weekly*: "The Real Story: How Angelina Tortures Jen," "What She Says About Jen Behind Her Back," "How She Got Naked on Set to Seduce a Married Brad," "Why Jen Refuses to Blame Brad for Her Pain ..."

Star Magazine: "Furious Brad: Shut Up, Jen!" "FINALLY REVEALED: The Real Reason Jen Wouldn't Have Brad's Baby ..."

In Touch: "Jen, I'm Sorry. Will It Erase Four Years of Jen's Hurt?" "Plus: Angelina's Furious They're Talking Again ..."

Even polite *Hello! Canada* joined the circus: "Life's a Beach for Jennifer Aniston as She Flaunts Her Flawless Physique and Opens Up About Men, ... Finally Admits to Having Harboured Resentment Toward Angelina Jolie."

On the next page is a photo of her ex and Jolie holding hands. Yeow, *Hello!*

On the cover of the December *Vogue*, Jen fairly sizzles in red on a beach as blonde as she is, and gripes: "What Angelina Did Was Very Uncool."

The capper, though, comes today. *GQ* hits most downtown newsstands, with Jen, 39, on the cover, coyly nude, except for a tie. It is a heady mix of space-age cosmetics, airbrushing, and aging star. Perhaps you have seen the preview. I bet Angelina has.

Jen insists there's no message behind the stunt, but you can hear the hisssss.

In case you have been dead or in Ottawa for the last three years, let me recap.

Jennifer and Brad married in 2000. We all swooned. Rosy days. Then al-Qaida, anthrax, George Bush, and Angelina Jolie came along, all deadly.

Angelina swept Brad off his smelly feet in 2005, they saved Africa and had 16 or 17 kids, including, what, four sets of twins? (I'm kidding.)

The supermarket tabs even reported Jen was having twins, too, just to get even. (I'm not kidding.)

The two women have glared at each other from checkout aisle shelves for years.

Jen has gone on revenge sleepovers with a comedian, a model, a singer, a tinker, tailor, soldier, sailor ...

Angie, 33, threw a fit after one of her kids arrived (I don't recall from where) when Jen sent over a nice fruit basket.

The latest flare-up? Angelina is ticked because Brad's mom is still palsy-walsy with Jennifer.

There hasn't been a catfight like this since Elizabeth I and Mary Queen of Scots. Or at least Tanya Harding and Nancy Kerrigan.

But is it real? I doubt it. I bet Brad, who is 45 today, Angie, Jen, and their agents lounge in the den every weekend, giggling at the rest of us, and plotting their next outrage.

"Say, Jenny, sweet, let's tell the *Enquirer* Brad's having twins."

Brad: "Well, yuck, yuck, it's every man's dream to have twins."

(Gales of laughter.)

Real or not, it sells. "They fly off the shelves," Tammy Robinson, 37, tells me at my Shoppers Drug Mart in Cliffcrest, where she stocks the magazine racks.

Tammy's a twin, so she's partial to Angelina, but she tries to stay neutral. "Maybe those two should get on with their lives," she says.

The rest of us, too, Tammy.

But no. There's an Angelina Camp and a Jennifer Camp. And it's Two Solitudes, North and South, dogs and cats.

You know if you are an Angelina Guy or a Jennifer Guy. Or Woman.

Just one of the many things that divide us in this troubled world.

This Beggar Has a Legal Beagle
(March 12, 2002)

Now I have seen everything. We are in a book-lined conference room on Bay Street. On the wall is a Norval Morrisseau original. I hate to think what it's worth.

At the head of a dark-stained table is a Bay Street lawyer, complete with navy pinstripes.

He is Leonard Hochberg, 35. He has called a press conference for his client, Margita Bangova, 66. She sits, jerking and sobbing, beside him.

The Shaky Lady.

Seven storeys below is Bay and Bloor. It is one of the Shaky Lady's favourite corners. Often, though not in the past few days, she has sat there, head and hands spasmodic. Mortified passersby gave her oodles of cash.

Down Bloor, at Yonge, I watched last week as she made at least $500 in five hours, then walked to meet her pickup car.

Now, through a translator and her Bay Street lawyer, the Shaky Lady tells us she makes only $40 to $50 a day.

Well, I talked to people who gave her that much in one go.

A TV reporter wonders: "She's being portrayed as a person in very difficult financial straits who has to beg on the streets, yet she can afford a (Bay Street) lawyer to plead her case...?"

Her Bay Street lawyer replies: "Don't you think everyone deserves the best lawyer they can get?"

Or can afford?

Actually, Hochberg has been her Bay Street lawyer since last summer. She hired him to help with her bid to become a landed immigrant. She has refugee status.

Now, he is doing damage control on her image.

This is no legal charity case. She pays her Bay Street lawyer, though he won't say how much.

Good grief, this is surreal. The Shaky Lady's purple-and-green knit top shines against the room's elegant wood.

Through her Bay Street lawyer, she wants us to know "she's very thankful for living in this country and has always appreciated the generosity of the people of this city."

Our donations are added to her $800 monthly social assistance and go towards the basics, she says through her Bay Street lawyer. That includes the $900, one-bedroom Scarborough apartment she shares with her husband, son, and three grandkids.

Son Lubomir, an unemployed landscaper, bought the apartment's big-screen TV, computer, and leather couches, she says through her Bay Street lawyer.

Lubomir, 29, is a large chap. I have seen him in his mother's pickup car, a Chevy Lumina.

The Shaky Lady tells us, through her Bay Street lawyer, that her shaking is from a thyroid condition.

She says, through her Bay Street lawyer, that the shaking eases when she is mobile. For instance, when she trots down the street to meet the Lumina.

She tells us, through her Bay Street lawyer, she had the thyroid condition before she arrived from the Czech Republic in 1997.

I remind her Bay Street lawyer of a video shot later that year in Toronto showing a shake-free Margita Bangova extolling Canada's virtues as a home for Gypsies.

The Shaky Lady, through her Bay Street lawyer, says she became allergic to medicine that controls the shakes.

I call my friend, Dr. Bernie Gosevitz. He has seen the Shaky Lady on the street and he watched her on TV yesterday.

"That is not a thyroid tremor," he tells me flatly. Thyroid tremors, he says, are fine and rapid, not grotesque.

"In 38 years of practice," says Dr. G., "I have never seen a thyroid tremor like that."

I will ask the Shaky Lady's Bay Street lawyer about that today.

The video also shows Margita's strong, straight hands, though now her fingers are bent and arthritic.

She tells us, through her Bay Street lawyer, that her family and other Gypsies were persecuted in her homeland, then called Czechoslovakia. She sobs.

Her Bay Street lawyer wraps up: "I would just like everyone to remember that charity blesses those who give as well as those who receive."

Warmth fills the room.

Then, a bit of a shocker. She says, through her Bay Street lawyer, she is considering returning to her street corners. She has to make a living, her Bay Street lawyer says.

"She really has no marketable skills. She's not putting money away, she's not making huge contributions to an RRSP, she's just living … day to day."

Like a lot of people I know.

Most of whom can't afford a Bay Street lawyer.

BOYS BEING BOYS

Porn Stardom — For a Price
(January 7, 2002)

"Ever been in adult films, Michael?" Leila Stephens asks. She is a casting director. We're in her cramped office in a tiny bungalow on Sheppard Avenue just west of Yonge.

No, I say, looking naive, I'm a farmer. Which is true, sort of.

"Ever had HIV?"

I look shocked that she would even ask.

She's 20 or so, raven-haired, dressed in black, including boots and a scoop-cut top.

She's typing, my answers presumably, at a huge monitor. She seems to be reading questions from a script.

"How will working in adult films change your life? Would you prefer to wear a mask when you perform? Have you thought of a stage name?"

Old Baldy? I suggest. She's impassive.

"Do you think you have the commitment to work in the adult film industry, Michael?"

Oh, yes, I say, looking keen.

"Congratulations," she beams, after the five-minute grilling. "I've decided to accept your application."

I beam back.

She says she has me in mind for a role in *Phys. Ed. 101*, which shoots in two weeks.

I'm perfect for the part of the professor.

She outlines the plot. Two coeds visit the professor in hopes of better marks. The rest, apparently, is improv.

"Do you think you are prepared for this kind of role, Michael?" Leila asks.

"Absolutely," I lie. "Born for it."

Out front, three other guys await their interviews. No one makes eye contact. The receptionist sits behind dark glass.

You enter the off-white bungalow through a red door. MQIS INC., says a sign. APPOINTMENT ONLY.

Muted club music fills the waiting room. Decor is North York Serengeti. Fake leopard and zebra rugs. Giraffe lamp. Soft lights. Dark green leather couches.

There's a poster of the Hollywood flick *Going All the Way*. If that doesn't get you in the mood, a TV shows hardcore porn movies.

In her office, Leila is explaining a few facts of life.

"You can't get into the adult film business," she says, "without a proper portfolio. Have you ever had nude photos taken of yourself, Michael?"

Gosh, no.

"No problem," beams Leila. She'll arrange a photo session with a young woman in the basement of the bungalow. The pictures will be my entree to the porn biz.

I can even pick my partner. Leila spins the huge computer screen toward me. Women flash before my eyes. I pick a tall blonde named Stacy. I once had a crush on a Stacy.

"I can arrange it for Monday," says Leila. "We take cash, cards, or Interac. It's $495." Plus tax.

I gulp like a startled farmer.

"I'll get back to you," I tell Leila.

So Carol Crosby was right about the photos, I think on the way out.

A call from Crosby, 51, of Durham, is why I'm applying for a porn job on a wintry weekend.

Crosby's son John, in Scarborough, and ex-husband Mitch, in Durham, each responded to an MQIS ad. They run in several papers, including this one. No experience, great income, it says. "Have fun working with gorgeous models."

John, 35, and stepdad Mitch, 41, bit. Each paid $500 for their portfolio shots. Nudity, but no sex.

John signed on for his first film — and paid $2,400. He says he was told it was an investment in the production.

Carol Crosby shakes her head. She has big blond hair. We're at a coffee shop off the 401 in Whitby.

"I love my son dearly," she says, "but he's not always the brightest bunny in the forest."

So John was filmed having sex with a young woman in a North York hotel room. Payment? He says they offered him 100 DVDs of the flick. In the contract's fine print, the DVDs cover salary and investment.

So you apply for a porn job — and you pay $2,900, pics and investment. You make your dough by re-selling the DVDs of yourself having sex. The contract does not suggest to whom to sell the DVDs. Presumably, not to close relatives.

Well, Carol's son is certainly the *toughest* bunny in the forest. He wears leather and silver studs. He marched into the little bungalow and browbeat them into returning his money.

Mitch, meanwhile, put $400 down and signed the contract. Then he showed it to Carol, with whom he lives platonically.

She went through the roof. On New Year's Eve she took Mitch down to Sheppard Avenue to demand his money back. They said no.

She gave four guys in the waiting room a lecture on reading contracts. Then she called me. Which brought me to Leila.

I arranged to meet Leila again yesterday — to identify myself and get a response to Carol Crosby's story.

But Leila didn't show. I told the receptionist, Mia, who I really was and asked her to get Leila or another company rep to call. As of deadline, no one had.

Fact is, MQIS does what it says it will do in its contract.

Maybe the best I can offer is this: open your eyes before you sign any contract, especially if you're thinking with a body part other than your brain.

Take it as wise advice. Hell, I was almost a professor.

We Are 50. Hear Us Croak.
(July 30, 2005)

In a few days I will be old. Cinquante. Funfzig. Wu shi. Cincuenta. Fifty. Five-O. Old.

I will be a quinquagenarian.

Gawd, get me a shrink. Dr. Irvin Wolkoff calls back. Perfect. My favourite shrink — and he became a quinquagenarian three years ago.

"Turning 50 is exactly the same as turning 14," he says, in that soothing shrink voice.

"It's just another passage of another calendar year. That's the fact. But you wanna know the truth?"

Please, doc.

"It's a HUGE milestone."

I know, I know. Forty was a minor jolt. Thirty, I don't even remember. Twenty, ah, 20. My head had more hair than my nose and ears.

But 50 ...

"I know. Even if you're a Nobel prize winner, you think you haven't done anything, that you've flushed 50 years."

The web says not to fret. It is full of cute ways to celebrate.

"Party with 50 friends for 50 days," says one site. "Go to restaurants, have them around for dinner, have breakfast together, go for lunch ... "

Then you will be old, fat, and broke. Anyway, who the hell has 50 friends?

I'm with Irvin. He hid in his room.

"I was pretty low. Refused to have a big party. Avoided people I'd known since I was 18. I had to convalesce from a face full of dashed hopes and broken dreams.

"I was gonna cure all mental illness by the time I was 50."

I'm so sorry, Irvin.

"It's tragic, Mike. But a month later I was fine. Now I really enjoy it. I have more authority in my world. I do stuff I really like, my wife's still great looking and she still thinks I'm the rumba man.

"Sure, sometimes I fall asleep on the couch at 7 o'clock, but that's okay. I'm 53."

His advice? Get a clear, *honest* picture in your head of who you are, what you've got, and what you will do.

And get a grip. "In this culture, at 50, you're still fairly young and in great shape."

Plus you can join some neat new groups. Lawn bowling clubs. Surgery support groups.

And Canada's Association for the Fifty-Plus. CARP. CARP?

"It used to be Canadian Association of Retired Persons," exec Judy Cutler, 64, tells me. "We kept the acronym."

Good, one less acronym to remember. The other day I was in the garage in the dark trying to recall why I was in the garage in the dark.

CARP is my new champion. I am the 400,001st member, or I will be after August 8 and I mail in my $19.95.

It gets me *50 Plus Magazine*, discounts on insurance, and such.

We are lobbying the Senate to study and combat ageism. If anyone knows about ageism, it is the Senate.

We are demanding those pups in Parliament reform pensions, health and home care, and toss mandatory retirement.

We are old. Hear us croak.

But, Judy, I do not feel old. Just a little tired. It does not help that I am on crutches for trying to play basketball with post-baby boomers.

Look who else turns 50 in August.

Elvis. Not THAT Elvis. Elvis Costello. He's sleeping with Diana Krall, for crying out loud.

Billy Bob Thornton. Bad Santa. Okay, Billy Bob is old.

Do not forget, we quinquagenarians are the beer-belly of the baby boom (9.4 million Canadians born 1946–64). We rule. In 30 years, one in four Canadians will be over 65.

Whoa, Judy, let's just get through 50. What was it like when you turned?

"I was more aware of my mortality, but I felt younger at 50 than at 40. I looked after myself, I was less stressed. It was more about how other people looked at me.

"Society is still youth-oriented. We hear from older workers who cheat on their resumes, taking out some of their experience so they don't seem old enough to have done all that.

"And there's billions of dollars in creams and other products to defy aging."

As CARP members, do we get great deals on that stuff?

"Oh, you're just a kid."

Thanks. You're right. I'm still only 49.

Where the Boys Aren't
(September 17, 2008)

Travel south of a man's belt buckle and you will find two of the great paradoxes of the English language.

What the heck should we call those things? The question has tormented men, and very few women, for eons.

Science refers to them as testicles.

But we men wince at that word, which sounds sharp and harsh, so we have concocted a variety of less threatening expressions.

The boys, for instance. Chestnuts, to lend a Christmasy touch. Or fric and frac, family jewels, slats, rocks, bollocks, Sandra Bullocks, Jackson Pollocks, jingleberries, bonbons, nuts, marshmallows, clappers, yongles, gonads, do-dads, love-apples, higgumbobs, mcnuggets, berries, crackerjacks, nackers, taters, acorns, sweets, swingers, gadgets, bean-bags and chuckles. To name a few.

Likely, you have your personal favourite.

The subject arises recently on three fronts. First, there's that Bud Light commercial featuring Bag O' Marbles, a poolside geek in a Speedo.

Then Florida bans a popular bumper ornament — metal bull's bobblers, called Truck Nutz.

And now the Sun Media Style Guide has arrived, to govern word use in our 43 dailies and 200-plus community papers across the country. That is no small potatoes, pardon the expression, since 6.4 million Canadians read us every week.

The new style guide is chockablock with gems. It lists the Seven Dwarfs, the seven seas and the seven wonders of the world. Now we know the proper spelling of brussels sprouts, aficionado (I always put two *f*s), amok, hors d'oeuvres and the difference between Mississauga, the city, and Massasauga, the snake.

But one rule has raised eyebrows across the chain. " 'Balls' (to describe testicles) needs approval of senior manager."

So we cannot write, without approval, "The right whale has the largest balls in the world, each weighing 500 kg, or 1,110 pounds."

Instead: "Wow, did you see the whirlygigs on Moby D---!?"

Of course, "balls" is OK in covering sports, especially baseball. And, with caution, we may use it as a synonym for gumption or courage. As in, "It takes a councillor with a lot of balls to stand up to Mayor Miller."

The style guide is authored by an old friend of mine, Marty "Huevos" Hudson, who's a honcho at our paper in Calgary, where the buffalo and prairie oysters roam.

Marty must be a fan of the late George Carlin, because now there are Seven Dirty Words off limits to *Sun* scribes.

Obviously, I cannot tell you what they are, even with senior management approval. But a couple rhyme with "trucker" and at least two are standard fare in the Bible.

Outside the Big Seven, some words can be hinted at, if in quotes and if important to the story: to wit: B-------, f---, s---, and a------.

Dash it all, that will be tough with a federal election going on.

I'm ashamed to say my columns have set a sorry example. Our archive claims I've written "damn" 108 times. Never the "f" word, though. Only one *Sun* writer has dared use it. Twice.

Not mentioning names. Eh, Mr. B--------?

Anyway, welcome to the newsroom chapter of the No Cussing Club. I reach club founder McKay Hatch at his home in suburban Los Angeles. McKay, 15, is in Grade 10.

Sickened by the cloud of profanity at his school, McKay started the No Cussing Club to much media fanfare last year. There are now 27,000 members worldwide. (See *nocussing.com*.)

"That's really, really cool," says McKay when I tell him of our new, unofficial chapter. "All newspapers should do it."

So "balls" is out? Even if it means courage?

"What's wrong with 'guts' or something like that?

"Cussing always starts with the little words and gets bigger and bigger. Newspapers shouldn't even get close to profanity. Nothing stronger than 'heck' or 'darn.'"

Already, McKay is carrying his message to other schools, and sees a future as a speaker.

Good for you, kid. Trying to clean up our world.

That takes real cojones.

Ewwww, Chest Hair!
(May 22, 2009)

Summer's here, so where are all the topless women?

Our streets, parks, and sidewalks should be teeming with them. They're not. I've looked everywhere. (But, Mikey, we can't allow that. It's indecent! Immoral! And illegal!)

Hey, keep your shirt on. You've forgotten the 1996 Ontario court of appeals ruling that women doffing their tops in public is just dandy.

But in the dozen years since, few women have taken advantage. I guess by the time they get around to thinking about it, it's already winter.

So, what are we left with?

Topless men. Oh, joy. Nothing says summer like a beefy, sweaty, sunburned, half-naked dude.

Worse, I've noticed an alarming trend among the Toms, Dicks, and Harrys who jog, rollerblade, or just generally preen on the byways of the Big Smoke.

WHERE DID ALL THE CHEST HAIR GO?

God did not intend the human male torso to be devoid of foliage. Yet stand a while on Queens Quay during a scorcher. The only male body hair you see is on the Chihuahuas.

I blame James Bond for this. The new version, Daniel Craig.

When he emerged shaven from the sea to canoodle with Eva Green in *Casino Royale*, evolution was complete. The last link to our ancestral apes went out of style.

Bye-bye bushy chests.

Women claim they're happy to see them go, though I suspect there's something akin to penis envy afoot.

Even my Mediterranean friend Irene turns up her nose. "Ewww, chest hair," she says. "And I'm Greek and married to a guy named Harry."

Poor Harry. Irene makes him wax for holidays.

Speaking of going south, the trend has spread to all of a man's nooks and crannies. Nary a follicle on a fella's physique is safe anymore. It's follicular homicide.

And I don't mean just on body builders and Chippendale dancers.

No, Medallion Man, with his gold chains and curlicue carpet, has gone the way of the Neanderthal.

Hirsute singer Tom Jones, who reportedly insured his manscape for $7 million, would be run out of town. So would Burt Reynolds, Joe Namath, the rock band Kiss, every 1970s porn star, Chuck Norris, and former Bonds Sean Connery and Pierce Brosnan.

Me, too, if I ever took off my shirt. Except in Little Italy, perhaps.

What a shame. Society has reached a sorry state if men feel they must shave, wax, laser, trim, or tweeze before venturing outside sans shirt.

I'm reading up on this, and it's gross. Bloody medieval. For instance, some men turn to "sugaring" off their overgrowth.

Sounds sweet, eh? Think again, buster.

Some sicko dominatrix, called an aesthetician, covers you in a paste of sugar, lemon, and citric acid.

Then she rips it off — taking hair, roots, and presumably moles, tattoos, jewellery, and bits of skin and flesh.

The ancient Egyptians invented this. The same folks who tortured foes with scorpions. I mean, kiss my asp.

Don't even ask me about electrolysis. Fingernail removal costs extra.

Enough, I say. It's sadistic. Women would never stand for such nonsense. Or would they?

Rise, my bushy brethren. Revel again in the sheer joy of the breeze rustling across your unshorn chest, down your back and into the deepest, darkest reaches of your topography.

Too late? Already plucked or waxed? Or did God sell you short, poor sap?

Then buy your way back to manliness. Surely, your flea market or memorabilia shop still sells fake chest rugs.

Perhaps you know a 1970s porn star who will lend you his. Whatever it takes.

Until women work up the nerve, we're the only topless show in town this summer.

So take off your shirt, puff out your chest and repeat after me ...

I am hairy, hear me roar.

Give Him an Inch, He'll Take a Smile
(April 8, 2002)

How big? I ask, frowning at the capsules in my hand.

"Up to 25% bigger than it is now," says the voice down the line.

"Permanently?"

"Oh, yes. It should take about three or four bottles."

"How will I know when to stop?"

"When you get to eight or nine inches," says the voice.

I choke back a chortle.

I'm on the phone with Irvin Turner, 68, an Oshawa herbalist. I'm holding a plastic bottle of his Eratos. It's new. He advertises it in our paper, and others. The brochure is quite something. It is even more eloquent than Turner himself about the results.

"Increase your penis size by 25%. This is our guarantee!" it says. Then, "measure yourself during full erection and add 25%. That is the average size increase."

A bit confusing. Average? Minimum? As much as? Still, it's an eye-popping promise, no matter how you slice it.

And not only will your penis be bigger, says Turner. "It will also be better looking."

Just what every guy wants. A penis that looks like Brad Pitt.

The brochure, by Turner's Carlisle Laboratories Inc., has some novel sales pitches. For one, it refers to a book called *97 Reasons White Women Prefer Black Men.*

I cannot find the book in the Sun library. Perhaps it is out.

Our lawyer is Alan Shanoff. I've affectionately called him Little Al for years. I won't call him that for this column.

Shanoff okayed Eratos for an ad after checking the listed ingredients. None are banned.

Not listed is an herb Turner calls bois bande. It means "strip of wood" and grows on such Caribbean isles as Antigua. Turner was born there. He came to Canada 23 years ago. Antiguan men have been taking bois bande for years. Turner says it prevents prostate cancer.

Not to mention its effect on your unmentionables.

I run the list of ingredients past pharmacist Marvin Malamed at Habers Pharmacy on Bathurst Street.

Most do influence the nether regions, Malamed, 59, tells me.

Nettle, pumpkin seed and saw palmetto, for instance, are good for prostates. Soy extracts weed out excess estrogen.

Ginger, oddly, is listed. It's good for the digestion. Perhaps that's for the candle-lit dinner before you try out your new equipment.

Malamed chuckles at the 25% growth claim.

So does plastic surgeon Dr. Robert Stubbs. He likely is the city's top penis repairman. His surgery can add 6 cm, tops. Say two inches. But a pill?

"Only three things will give you a bigger penis (aside from surgery)," says Stubbs, who studied with a Dr. Long in China: (1) Heredity, (2) Testosterone shots before age two, (3) Hanging rocks from it, like some monks do in India. It becomes a foot long, but is as useful as an elastic band.

"All men want bigger," says Stubbs, 52. "It's psychologically ingrained. The biggest guy always ruled the herd or the family. So if they think they can just take a pill … they'll buy it."

Uh, you ever expanded on nature yourself, Dr. Stubbs?

"No, no," he laughs. "My wives have always been more concerned about the bulge in my back pocket."

You sure will need a wad of dough for Eratos. Each bottle of 70 capsules is $78.

You pop two capsules daily. "Also, after taking your shower in the morning, hold your penis by the glans (tip) and stretch it for a few minutes," says the pamphlet.

Hey, that's cheating.

In one to four weeks, "your penis will become greater and longer with lasting erections and an obvious increase in thickness."

In 10 weeks it "will be harder, healthier, longer, thicker and will have a new appearance." (Say hello to Mr. Pitt?)

We'll see. As a consumer service, I'm taking the stuff.

So far, nothing. Except I think my hair is growing back. Well, Rome wasn't well-built in a day.

I'm assured the ingredients are safe. Testing seems a bit iffy. "We gave it to a few men who used it and observed the tremendous benefits," says Turner.

You use it, Mr. Turner?

"Oh, yes. I've noticed a greater size and more thrusting power." Jeez, maybe someone should tell NASA about this.

The capsules smell funny. Turner says that's the saw palmetto and thyme.

Anyway, I'll let you know how it goes.

Assuming I can get out from behind my desk.

Beauty Tips for Your Beast
(December 7, 2006)

"What the heck is that?" says the other side of the bed.

She is peering at my neck.

"What? What?! Holy cow, what?"

"I think it's a wattle."

"A what?"

"A wattle." And she goes back to reading a book with a pirate on the cover. The pirate is shirtless. And wattle-less.

Women can be so cruel when you are 50.

So I dream of roosters and wattles and wrinkles and wake up in a cold sweat only to read that some dame is on Mick Jagger's case, too.

Sir Mick, 63 and prune-like, has taken to caviar face cream to counter all those years of depravity.

L'Wren Scott, his girlfriend, is said to be delighted. Lucky for Mick. L'Wren, 39, is a 6-foot-4 Mormon with hard eyes.

Bandmate Keith Richards, 62, has been given a gift of the protein-rich cream. And a trowel, I hope.

Then I read where *Consumer Reports* says even the best anti-aging creams reduce the depth of wrinkles by less than 10%, barely noticeable.

The $20 creams work as well (or as poorly) as $400 creams. What's a wrinkly wretch to do?

When in doubt, I always turn to jowly Jimmy Buffett. *And wrinkles only go where the smiles have been.*

Or where the sun don't shine. Some folks swear by Preparation H to shrink wrinkles. The Canadian version is especially popular, even in the States, since it also contains a yeast extract to soothe skin.

My ass. Why bother?

Why are we men dragged into the whole Nivea nightmare?

Why has the men's lotions and potions industry doubled in the past decade?

Why is men's cosmetic surgery outpacing women's? Why are "gentle exfoliants" for women re-emerging as "face scrubs" for men? Vanity, thy name is man?

Forget it, boys.

Let's worship the ground Robert Redford ambles upon. Watch *Butch Cassidy and the Sundance Kid*, then take a gander at him now.

Wattles to his knees and women still swoon.

"I'm not a facelift person," he tells *TV Guide*. "I am what I am. The trade-off is that something of your soul in your face goes away. You end up looking body-snatched.

"That's just my view. It's not necessarily a popular view."

No, sad to say. And, ahem, let's not mention that miraculous blonde mane.

While we're at it, look at Butch, look at Paul Newman. Crinkly as rice paper, yet hot as a pistol at 81.

Or Gordon Pinsent. That dimple has disappeared in his chin, yet there he is starring in a new movie with Julie Christie, the sexiest woman who ever lived.

Nor have wrinkles hurt Gordon Lightfoot or Neil Young, Sean Connery or Donald Sutherland,

So why the pressure on us regular jowly joes?

"Ageism," says Dave Lackie, editor of *Cosmetics Magazine*. "Men who look younger, more vibrant are getting the leg up for promotions over men who look older.

"And we're starting to see objectification of men in advertising. Men with that six-pack look."

Hey, I have a six-pack. I keep it in the fridge.

"Not that kind. I mean well-defined abs."

And there's the Baby Boom, now in its gnarly years.

"From the neck down they're 60, but from the neck up

they see themselves as 30. Then they look in the mirror."

This tragedy strikes later for men. Our thicker, oilier, hairier skin protects us for a while.

Lackie, 39, is a La Roche-Posay cream man, but he says a good sunscreen is your best ticket to the fountain of youth.

Smoking, drinking, stress, eating too much, pollution, squinting, dust, and many other things turn you into a raisin.

Life, in other words.

"There is much to be said for aging gracefully," says Lackie.

You can get a facelift or botox, but that requires upkeep and you might look like Phyllis Diller.

Earthier remedies include emu oil, egg whites, seedless grapes, and crushed pearls.

Or, try this: Never, ever smile. Your face will stay smooth as a baby's bum. Of course, you will have no friends, to bask in your glow.

What's a wattle or two, just among us chickens?

We Fake Love, Commitment. Orgasms?
(October 19, 2006)

I see the annual Fake Orgasm Contest is upon us. Starts tomorrow at the Automotive Building, of all places.

Flush your fuel line? Put a little unleaded in your pencil?

The focus naturally will be on female fakers.

As my colleague Val Gibson told us last week, fellas, 70 percent of women are pulling our leg.

Canadian women are among the best at this, apparently.

"If you can't have one and the guy's trying really hard, why make him feel bad?" 2003 champion Zhanna Yampolsky once told me. "Why let him work for hours and hours and nothing happens?"

So sweet. So considerate. So Canadian.

But what of us Johnny Canucks? We fake love. We fake enthusiasm. We fake commitment. Hell, I've faked entire relationships. Do we fake orgasms?

"Impossible," says my friend Dave, who has a wife half his age and always looks tired.

Even the guy who runs Aren't We Naughty is skeptical.

"Naaw," says Jim Terkalas, 50, the chain's GM. "How can you? There's evidence. It's like leaving a business card."

So, Jim, you, uh, ever ...?

"Never. I don't understand why any man would."

Well, maybe he's sleepy. Or stressed. Or drunk. Or his wife is expecting him home for dinner. Or the Leafs game is on TV in five minutes.

Jim and Dave are just bluffing, I think. No sense showing your gender's whole hand in the game of *amore*.

The fact is men fake it. Or, 20 percent of us admit we fake it sometimes, according to polls.

Good. Tit for tat. What's good for the goose....

Women have been driving us nuts for eons. Was it real? All that yipping and yowling? Did you really make her faint? Or feign?

It is a test of our manhood, never mind the assurances of sex columnists.

"One of these days, Alice," Jackie Gleason used to say, "pow, zam, I'm gonna send you to the moon."

We all knew what he meant.

But males? Hey, our booster rocket's on automatic.

"Men are supposed to be raring to go anytime, anyplace," Josey Vogels tells me from her Parkdale home. "My Messy Bedroom" is her syndicated advice column.

Yesterday was her 42nd birthday. I hope she saw fireworks.

"There is incredible performance pressure on men," she tells me. I'm surprised they don't fake it even more than women.

"In our culture, women are expected not to be orgasmic. Everyone knows it's more difficult for them."

Plus, for a guy, faking it is less demanding a performance. Even a simple grunt might suffice.

A couple of years ago, two men entered Halifax radio station CFRQ-FM's fake orgasm contest. One b-a-a-a-ed like Mary's lamb. The other cried "J'arrive!"

A listener complained to the broadcast standards people. Juvenile, maybe, but hardly realistic, a panel ruled.

So, gentle women, if your feller bleats like a sheep or suddenly spouts French, he is not shooting straight.

Same if the performance goes on and on and on.

"As you know," says Vogels, "for guys it's a very quick ramp up, a few seconds at most, then a quick ramp down.

"Then your brain switches off. You want to sleep or you want a sandwich."

Other signs of the real deal: flared nostrils and flushing of skin where blood is close to the surface, such as lips and earlobes.

"You usually know when someone is caught up in the moment," says Vogels. "And it's harder to fake it with a partner who really knows you."

Be suspicious if he looks like he's doing pushups in the gym. Or he stares blankly at the wall mirror. Or he prays. Or counts backwards from 100. Or hums the *Hockey Night in Canada* theme.

Do not fall for the myth that we cannot, do not, fake it.

There is a reason most magicians are men. We are masters at slight of hand. That condom, for instance? Now you see it, now you don't.

An erection is not always a clue, says Vogels. "Sometimes that's just hydraulics."

And as you know, ladies, we are a wary, uncommunicative bunch.

So, few if any of us will mount the stage at the Automotive Building, during the Everything to do with Sex Show, through Sunday.

No male has ever won the Fake Orgasm Contest, or even come close. Why give away our secrets?

Keep 'em guessing.

BUREAUCRAP!

Rudolph Must Die!
(May 4, 2008)

Dear Santa: I hope you are sitting down — the Toronto Zoo is killing baby boy reindeer.

Now Dasher! Now Dancer! Now Prancer ...

The first was dispatched shortly after his birth April 8. His mom, Hayzel, bellowed mournfully for two days. You could hear her from Meadowvale Road.

The second met the same fate at the point of a hypodermic on April 22.

His mom, CUPE, is named for the zoo staff's union.

Both little gaffers were chocolate brown and gangly cute. They had barely begun to nurse.

Both were perfectly healthy.

"Euthanized due to being male," says the keepers' report, terse and angry.

The keepers were so upset they left as the vets moved into the reindeer enclosure and refused to take part.

"This is wrong," the keepers told the vets, who were none too happy either.

Three female babies have been spared.

Tinsel and Rhonda delivered their calves the same day as CUPE.

Lucky for them, they had girls, now prancing about the paddock in the full flush of spring.

Girl European reindeer are less hassle. Easier to sell or trade to other zoos. I'm told they're even better at hauling a sleigh.

Two years ago, zoo execs gave approval in principle to the euthanizing of male reindeer. This spring is the first time it's been executed, so to speak.

Remarkable, eh? I wonder if anyone considered how this looks. Call it herd management, or whatever. They're snuffing Rudolph.

They never let poor Rudolph
join in any reindeer games

Never before has the zoo imposed an euthanasia order on a breed of large animal. The only precedent I can find, about five years back, is the mara, a sort of jumping guinea pig from South America.

The zoo euthanized male maras to cap the population. Later, it sold off the whole lot.

Many staff wonder: Why kill the boy reindeer? Why not just neuter them?

True, this can cause atrophied antlers. Big deal. The kiddies who visit will still ooh and ahhh and hum "Jingle Bells."

Or, staff wonder, if you're going to exterminate every male, why breed the eight females in the first place?

Seems rather cruel. Reindeer roulette. Female, you live. Male, you die.

Says one staffer: "This bothers me more than anything I've ever experienced here.

"Many of us feel these are not our animals and not management's animals, but belong to the city, to the people of Toronto.

"And they should know what's happening."

Says another: "I'm sick to my stomach. This is the beginning of a road we don't want to go down."

Funny, I thought zoos love baby animals. There's always a fuss when a cute little snow leopard or polar bear comes into the world, out in the wilds of northeast Scarborough.

Two days before Hayzel's son was put to death with sodium pentobarbital, a press release announced the arrival of a baby gaur.

Congratulations to Flower and Hercules. Gaurs are huge, wild Asian cattle. The baby? A bouncing boy. Doing fine.

Need I add, a week from now is Mother's Day at the zoo. Given what's transpired, I hope they have the sense not to showcase the reindeer moms. Two of them aren't celebrating.

Maria Franke, curator of mammals, tells me the decision to euthanize male reindeer calves was made by something called the Animal Care, Research and Acquisition Committee.

"It was a gruelling process," she assures me. "We do not take this lightly. There is science behind it."

It's especially hard to sell reindeer because of disease fears. There's no room. Too expensive to release in the wild. If they keep the males they'll be lonely. They yearn for their own harem. We can't even sell the two bucks we have now. No one likes this. It's a necessary evil. Blah, blah, blah.

You're killing baby reindeer!

So why breed the herd, knowing half the babies are doomed?

"If we did not, we would end up with no reindeer," says Franke. "We aren't just an entertainment facility. We're a conservation facility and our goal is to manage genetically viable populations of animals.

"I know some keepers are upset. I know it's a sensitive subject."

No kidding. Just wait'll word gets back to the North Pole.

And it's not over. One more calf is due any day now.

We're all hoping for a girl.

The Hardy Genus *Dufus Bureaucratis*
(May 7, 2008)

Now that the Toronto Zoo has euthanized two baby reindeer, I assume space has opened up for other species.

One breed in particular is always looking for a home: *Dufus bureaucratis.*

This is a wide-ranging and hardy genus, with a vivid variety of sub-species, bird, and beast. In the column racket, you cross paths with a menagerie of these critters.

One, a young Truncated Bark Borer (*Politicolis correctus*), insisted to me that City Hall's Christmas tree be called a "holiday tree."

Illustration by Pam Davies/SUN MEDIA.

A relative, a Small-Tailed Shrew (*Feminis fanatica*) barred Miss Universe from Nathan Phillips Square.

Then, a college student with no arms and no legs was denied a Wheel-Trans Pass by a Purple Transitory Form Checker (*Duplicatus officialium*).

No doubt you have encountered one or all of these in the wild.

Some members of the *bureaucratis* genus are classified as parasites or pests, much like locusts, earwigs, telemarketers, and Africanized killer bees.

Others are brave and desirable, not to mention endangered. They are kings and queens of the civil service Serengeti.

Lately, the zoo has several species on display. But they are everywhere.

How do you tell them apart as you hack through the jungle of daily life?

Here is a field guide:

Ignor amus myopica. Commonly known as the Short-Sighted Ass and closely related to the donkey, though most donkeys deny the link.

In the wild, *Ignor amus myopica* cannot see the forest for the trees. Thus, out of fear, it invariably follows the same well-worn trail.

The beast is distinguished by bruises on its forehead, from bumping into the next Short-Sighted Ass up the path.

Often spotted hovering above *Ignor amus myopica* is its avian cousin, the Natty-Breasted Nitpicker (*Nocandu nowae nohow*).

It is a chatty git, noted for its piercing cry, "to-wit, to-wit, to-wit." As in, "this cannot happen for many reasons. To wit … "

Its opposite in the *bureaucratis* kingdom is the Stone-Faced Lummox. This beast is immovable and unshakable.

No matter how much you explain, shout, demand, curse, beg, weep, or whimper, it does not change its stance or expression. It knows it is right, and to hell with the rest of us animals.

It can justify anything, even the killing of healthy newborn reindeer.

The Yellow-Bellied Booby (*Covvermie buttus*) is among the more amusing types of *Dufus bureaucrati*.

A cross between a turtle and a quail, it has hawkish eyes, yet sees nothing, bat-like ears yet hears nothing, a foxy brain yet knows nothing.

"Hoomee? Hoomee? Hoomee?" is its plaintive cry, often followed by a pointing of its wing at a poor fellow denizen of the forest.

Others in this line of the family include the Lily-Livered Yak (*Gossipia internetus*), the Great Grasping Albatross (*Taxus roundour nex*), the Common Slug, the Committee Raccoon, which washes its hands of everything, the venomous Snake-in-the-Grass, the Northern Shoveler, the Corporate Ostrich, the Telephone Grouse, the Three-martini Sapsucker, the Mandarin Lemming, and the Ruffled Parrot.

The Wind-Blown Newt is identified by its chirpy call, after the guano has hit the fan: "I newt, I newt, I newt. I didn't dewt."

But the animal kingdom is yin and yang. For every hyena there is a lion. For every vulture, a golden eagle.

The genus *Dufus bureaucratis* is no exception. For instance, the Good Tern believes one deserves another and does its job accordingly. Likewise, the Golden-Headed Straight Shooter, *Honorabis erectum*, is upright and helpful.

Keep a sharp eye for the Splendid Ruby-throated Whistle-blower (*Publicus interestus*).

This noble animal is often solitary, but will travel in groups for protection. Threatened by those higher on the food chain, it often hides in underbrush, then fearlessly ventures outside its territory to sound alarms.

The Whistle-Blower has overcome its instinctive fear of Newshounds and Media Jackals, scruffiest and most unpredictable of beasts.

Thank goodness. Otherwise, the boobies, baboons, and cuckoos would take over the world.

No Arms, No Legs, No Bus Pass
(September 24, 2005)

The TTC has turned down Rafael Reyes, 23, for a Wheel-Trans Pass.

That is surprising, to say the least. Rafael Reyes, as you can clearly see in the photograph, has NO ARMS AND NO LEGS.

Gawd, I wish I was making this up.

Rafael is a medical engineering intern at Bloorview MacMillan Children's Centre. That is a wonderful haven for disabled kids just south of Sunnybrook.

Rafael knows about being a disabled kid. His mom slipped into a coma after a car accident and he was born with stumps for limbs. Nothing is wrong with his brain.

As an undergrad in Mexico City, his research included such things as "rehabilitation engineering" and "sensor design and artificial perception for robotics." In other words, he wants to help people like himself get around. The internship is the last notch in his degree.

Rafael got here August 19, 2005, on a student visa from Mexico, among a handful of foreign interns at the centre.

Three from Mexico settled in a basement apartment at Bloor and Christie. Then they helped Rafael down to old Metro Hall to apply for Wheel-Trans.

How else was he supposed to get around? Did I mention? He has NO ARMS AND NO LEGS.

Rafael does have hooks for arms and metal legs, on which he can lurch along. And a skateboard. Friends push him.

In the apartment, sans limbs, he sort of flops about. A roomie carries him up and down the stairs to the street.

Seems a no-brainer for a Wheel-Trans Pass.

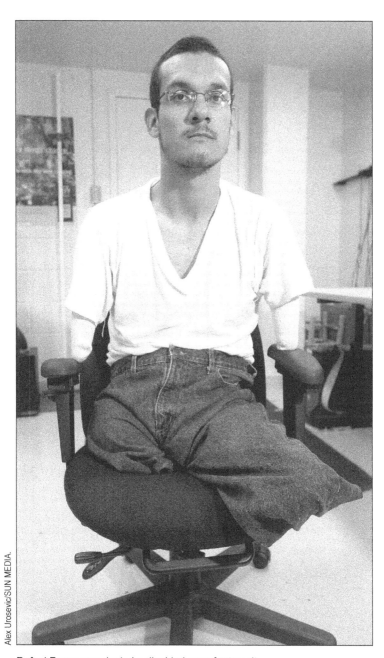

Alex Urosevic/SUN MEDIA.

Rafael Reyes was denied a disabled pass for transit.

A TTC lady interviewed him for 20 minutes. I assume she lifted her eyes off her questionnaire long enough to see who sat in front of her.

"We'll be in touch," she told Rafael. And off he lurched.

A week later, their response came by mail: "Your application for Wheel-Trans service has been denied."

Here's why. And this is bureaucracy in full blossom.

Rafael was rejected because he scored 0 out of 90 on the key question of whether he needs an "assistive device" to get around. List includes guide dog, neck or limb brace, walker, wheelchair, scooter, and, believe it or not, a stretcher.

I score 30 points because I'm on crutches (sore ankle).

Sadly for Rafael, nowhere on the form does it say "skateboard" or "roomie's back" or "HE HAS NO ARMS AND NO LEGS!" So, zero points.

The licence lady did not miss everything. "Awkward gait," she noted. "Uses no assistive device. (Cannot hold on to a cane or walker)."

Now there's a brilliant reason to reject. Too handicapped to hold a cane.

"I was absolutely appalled," says scientist Dr. Tom Chau, 35, Rafael's supervisor at the centre. "What impression does this give of Canada, or Toronto, that we can't even provide him with basic transportation?"

Chau has fired off a letter to the TTC.

Bureaucrats are not easily swayed, but I hope a politician gets wind and says, "Hey, this doesn't look good."

Meanwhile, Rafael takes up to two hours to get to the centre.

For instance, he has to lurch, or skateboard, all the way to the Bathurst Street subway. Christie Station is closer but not accessible. Then he hopes for one of those regular TTC buses with the moveable steps, then he lurches 600 metres from Eglinton Avenue to the centre.

It hurts me just thinking about it. Rafael already has missed a week with blisters on his stumps.

And winter?

Well, shudder, he has seen snow only on top of mountains, let alone had to get around in it.

"I'll have to trade my skateboard for a snowboard," he grins.

The guy takes everything in stride, pardon the expression. Friends call him Halfman. In Mexico City, his rock band (he figured out a way to play bass) is called 2 1/2. Guitarist, drummer, and Rafael.

But not even such humour and spirit can conquer the snowy, icy streets of Toronto.

Ever hear how a society is judged by how it treats its kids or its elderly? Or even its pets?

Well, it can be judged, too, by how it treats a visitor with NO ARMS AND NO LEGS.

(Note: Rafael Reyes got his pass the day after this column appeared.)

Yule Laugh, Too
(November 21, 2002)

A big green pointy thing has risen from Nathan Phillips Square. It has needles and bark and soon it will be covered in lights. But do not call it a Christmas tree.

No, no, no, no, no. It is City Hall's Official Holiday Tree.

You mean "Christmas tree," right? I ask Amber Authier, in the special events department, after I see the press release.

"No, 'holiday tree,'" she says, carefully and firmly. We're the city and we like to make sure people of all religions feel included in the festivities.

"We chose to be more inclusive this year, to make a concerted effort to make sure everyone feels it's their tree."

So you got complaints when you called it the Official Christmas Tree?

"I don't know of any complaints," says Authier, 29. "It was just us trying to be more inclusive."

I trot down to the tree. It is 52 feet tall. White spruce, from Toryville, near Haliburton.

Its branches have settled since Monday, so Arnold Huber, 37, has started stringing blue and white lights.

There will be 7,000 bulbs this year, down from 10,000. The hydro problems, you know.

The press release has other neat tree stats.

A crew of four, including Huber, from a display company will spend three days on decorations. Unlike an indoor tree, this one doesn't need watering.

When it's done, it will be recycled into mulch for walkways and flowerbeds.

Not once in the slick press package does the term "Christmas tree" appear. Well, I guess, if people were offended ...

I call my friend Little Al Shanoff, who is Jewish and wise beyond his 50 years.

"Offended? Of course not," he says. "It's a Christmas tree. What else are you gonna call it?"

I ring up Mohammad Zahid at the Muslim Association of Canada.

"Ridiculous," he chuckles. "I don't think sensitivity should go that far. Christmas trees are not offensive to us. I'm more offended by the commercialization of the occasion."

Well, you're not alone, Mohammad. But ever hear any Muslims complain about the ol' Official Christmas Tree?

"No, not one. I preach at the mosque that Canada is a unique experiment in the history of humanity. So many people from different religions and countries living together, while maintaining their cultural diversity."

Exactly. Nothing to do with trees. Besides, the Christmas tree's roots are pagan, not Christian.

Zahid is still chuckling as we hang up.

I can't find anyone who thinks "Christmas tree" might offend and should be banned.

Until, believe it or not, I call the Christmas Tree Farmers of Ontario.

"We agree with 'holiday tree,'" says Mary Anne Hough, from HQ in Wasaga Beach. She edits the farmers' newsletter, Ontario Christmas Tree News. "We've changed our whole focus from the 'Christmas season' to the 'holiday season,'" she says.

So, why aren't you the Holiday Tree Farmers of Ontario?

"We really can't change the name of our product. What would people think?"

So isn't that thing at City Hall a honking big Christmas tree?

"Well, it is, but we would call it a symbol of the festive season. Our society is now so multicultural that we don't want to be specific to the Christian religion."

Any flak about the old name?

"We have had absolutely no complaints."

Could Easter be the next to fall? Meet the Holiday Bunny?

"I don't know," Hough laughs. "You'll have to call the egg marketing board."

I'm surprised tree farmers are so politically correct. But they once reprinted an entire educational package because someone objected to the sexist "mankind" instead of "humankind."

Back under the tree, trimmer Arnold Huber and I have a rousing debate about multiculturalism. We're both all for it.

"But," he says, "why pick on the tree? They're so careful, bending over backwards not to offend anybody.

"And I don't think anybody's offended."

Of course not. It's just a Christmas tree, for crying out loud.

(Note: The name was changed back to Official Christmas Tree the next day.)

Battle Royale over Swimsuit Troops
(August 21, 2004)

Some days, you just want to crawl into a foxhole and cover your head.

We get a letter from National Defence in Ottawa: "IMMEDIATELY CEASE." The command is underlined in boldface.

What? What? What have we done? Has Peter Worthington let slip a military secret? Did we misspell Ypres?

No, says the letter. Much worse. The *Sun*, it says, has violated paragraph 291(1)(c) of the National Defence Act, section 419 of the Criminal Code of Canada, and subparagraph 9(1)(n)(i) of the Trade-Marks Act.

Oh, my. We're cooked. It's the brig for us.

Say, does the brig get copies of *Sun* swimsuit issues? Not in this man's army. Not anymore.

That's what the letter this week is about. DND is ticked that we used bits of uniforms, including caps and badges, in our 2004 Winter Swimsuit Edition.

Six months later, three (3) soldiers have complained and, voila, cease-and-desist.

The order was given by Major Jim McKillip. He is DND's Deputy Inspector of Badges and Insignia.

"I'm the guy who makes sure the use of badges, flags, uniforms and ceremonies corresponds with appropriate regulations," he tells me down the line from Ottawa.

That swimsuit edition, apparently, did not correspond.

To wit: on the cover, Julie dangled a naval officer's cap from a shapely foot. In the centre spread she wore the cap on her head, while saluting with Lynne (airman's cap) and Jessie (army beret).

Julie reappears 13 pages later in bewitching fishnet stockings and a 48th Highlanders cap.

The 48th Highlanders complained?!?

"No," says Major McKillip.

So, who did, then?

"The three complaints were from men and women here in Ottawa ... with concerns about the nature of some of the images."

But there's nothing you can't see on any beach. You don't think this is overreaction?

"Well, no, or I wouldn't have pursued it in the first place. Suggesting an association between pin-up girls and the Canadian Forces is just not something we're willing to do."

Funny thing, the only slightly raunchy image is Julie, again, draped in a strap or two of combat webbing, a canteen, and a helmet. But that's okay, says McKillip, because you can't tell that it's Canadian Forces.

Same for Jessie in a pillbox cap that might be a cadet's — or a Park Plaza doorman's.

"You can get this stuff at any army surplus," says our photographer, Silvia Pecota. Her makeup guy, Gig, found a sailor's cap at a dollar store before heading to St. Vincent and the Grenadines for the swimsuit photo session.

Silvia is dumbfounded by DND's reaction. The military is a specialty. Her website includes a tribute to our fallen in Afghanistan.

"I used parts of uniforms in the swimsuit issue because I wanted a 1940s look and because I wanted to bring attention to our soldiers. All my friends in the army loved it. I mean, I got the 48th Highlanders cap from a retired captain. Whoever complained should take a valium."

Our lawyer, Little Al Shanoff, smiles and tells me he hasn't seen the likes since Bill Clinton's people complained when we ran a Bad Boy ad with a Slick Willie lookalike.

"DND says it's bad for morale. If I was a soldier, I don't think this would have my morale flagging."

Al says the letter's legal claims are too broad, if you will pardon the expression, to stand up in court.

But who wants to joust with DND? We've always been fans of our armed forces. So, after today, we'll try not to use specific Canadian badges and such.

I don't think our troubles end there, though.

On page 15 of that swimsuit edition, Jessie was stunning in a two-piece and a pirate's hat.

Uh-oh.

> To: Toronto Sun
> From: Captain Kidd ...

Queen Meets Dukes of Duh!
(July 19, 2005)

This heat must be frying brains at City Hall. How else to explain the banning of Miss Universe from Nathan Phillips Square?

Yes, you read that right.

Strobel and Miss Universe Natalie Glebova. The crutches are courtesy of a basketball injury.

Natalie Glebova, 23, Toronto's own queen of the world, was to star at the Tastes of Thailand festival on the weekend.

The Thais are very big on Natalie. She won the Miss

Universe title in Bangkok seven weeks ago. Thailand made her an honorary ambassador.

Beauty pageants may have waned here. But Miss Universe is mobbed on many streets of the world.

And she is from Jarvis St. and Carlton, for crying out loud.

What a golden promo op for City Hall.

The Thais were into it. They had a press conference last week to announce Miss Universe will open the festival on the square. They put out a release.

They must have forgotten that some bureaucrats can read.

Prayoth Benyasut, deputy director of the Thai Trade Centre, got a call from City Hall's special events office.

Check the rules of the square, the supervisor Marguerite Reid tells him.

So, he does.

No hard liquor. Check.

No monkeys or venomous reptiles. Check.

No candles. Check.

No elephants. Well, it's Thailand, but ... check.

No loose helium balloons. Check.

Then: "Activities which degrade men or women through sexual stereotyping, or exploit the bodies of men, women, boys or girls solely for the purpose of attracting attention, are not permitted on Nathan Phillips Square."

There, says Ms. Reid. Natalie is a Miss Universa non grata.

She can come. But no sash, no tiara.

Do not introduce her as Miss Universe or even as a beauty queen. The bylaw says you must call her "an individual of note contributing to our community." Lovely. Here she is ... Miss Individual Of Note Contributing To Our Community.

Not surprisingly, Natalie and the Thais took a pass.

"It is quite weird," Benyasut says of City Hall's snub. "She is beautiful and talented and smart. She is nothing to be shy about."

He says there were hints the fest might have trouble with future permits if the Thais did not toe the line this time.

"I felt uncomfortable," the envoy says, then turns diplomatic. "We don't know the concept or the reason behind this, but we have to respect the laws and regulations of your country."

Well, this bylaw is an ass.

"It was like a knife in the heart," Natalie tells me, midway through a fashion magazine shoot.

"I'm travelling the world. I'm an ambassador for Toronto. I'm promoting Toronto. I love Toronto dearly. It seemed so silly. Everywhere else, I get great reaction from political leaders. But my hometown?"

Montreal's politicians, for instance, welcomed her. The mayor of her birthplace on the Black Sea in Russia has sent invites. City halls everywhere roll out the carpet.

Tastes of Thailand raised funds for tsunami relief. It also marked 60 years in the reign of King Bhu.

"It seemed a perfect fit," Miss Universe Organization president Paula Shugart tells me from New York. "She has a strong connection to Thailand. This was an insult not only to Natalie, but to the Thais.

"I have never been in a situation where someone has gone out of their way to uninvite a Miss Universe title holder."

Ms. Reid does not wish to discuss this with me. Nor does the other bureaucrat she passed me to. But soon I hear from media relations guy Brad Ross.

Brad, this is the dumbest thing I've seen all month.

"What I can say, officially, is as long as this bylaw is on the books, it's enforced. Maybe someone was following the letter of the law and people can't be faulted for that. What needs to happen is that council would have to amend that bylaw."

And say sorry to Miss Universe and the Thais, if you ask me.

(Note: Mayor David Miller rescinded the ban the next day and met with Ms. Glebova.)

The Nightmare Across the Street
(August 24, 2006)

Enter a nightmare on Graham Crescent. Chapter II is a doozie. But first, put yourself in Chapter I:

You are 15, going on 16. It's a quiet Saturday. You're tinkering with your mini-motorcycle in your garage in a leafy part of Markham.

Your two sisters are upstairs getting ready to visit grandma. Your mom, a paramedic, is sleeping off a night shift.

You glimpse a neighbour you barely know walking across the street. You think he is coming to admire the tiny bike, which you bought with your part-time Toys "R" Us wages.

You do not know he is hearing voices and carrying a black-handled fishing knife.

You are lucky. You can leave this nightmare. Young Nicolas Lastoria could not.

He looks up again. This time he sees the knife. The neighbour says nothing, just yanks the boy up by his T-shirt.

"What are you doing?" Nicolas asks. Again and again and again and again, the knife plunges into him, so violently, the handle bends right over.

In shock, Nicolas finally fends off the man and staggers away. Not to the house, for fear of drawing danger to his mom and sisters, but up the street to a driveway full of cars.

Halfway there, he hears, feels, air escaping a hole in his side. One of his lungs has burst. You know this if your mom is a paramedic.

He cannot breathe. For a minute, he cannot see.

Someone calls 911. The York Regional Police arrests Peter Galanos, 32, in the house across the street, where he lives with his parents.

Young Nicolas is in critical condition for two days at Sunnybrook. He goes home just before he turns 16 on May 2.

Nightmare on Graham Crescent: Chapter II.

"They've let him go," a detective at the door tells Nicolas' mom Elsa Ferraro, 45, last week. "He's home."

Sure enough, there he is, across the street from a kid he knifed nearly to death barely three months earlier. A shrink said he's okay so long as he takes his meds for paranoia-schizophrenia. Last Monday a judge agreed and found him "not criminally responsible" for the attack. And turned him loose.

A bewildered Nicolas, scars still red, paces his house for hours, peering across the street.

This is a good kid. "Life wouldn't be the same if Nicolas wasn't so generous," says his yearbook.

"How could they do this?" he asks his mom. "He almost killed me and he's back across the street already. How can I live like this?"

The next day she sends him to stay with his dad a while.

"I didn't know what to say to him," Elsa tells me. "I had no answers."

And she is still waiting for them.

She wants to see the Whitby psych report on Galanos. She wants to know why she wasn't notified of the hearing last Monday. What about a victim impact statement? Did the judge, the shrinks, know the attacker was a neighbour?

WHY THE HELL IS THIS GUY STILL ACROSS THE STREET?

Elsa sees awful things on her job, including one doomed, stabbed teen.

"You always think, 'when is it my family's turn?' Then it happens in my own garage. If my kids cannot feel safe in their own home, where can they feel safe?"

She stares across at the Galanos' tidy, two-storey house.

"I'm a prisoner in my own house," she says. She locks all doors, draws all blinds by 7:00 p.m.

The judge's "not criminally responsible" verdict automatically sends the file to the Ontario Review Board. The board can send Galanos to a psych hospital. Seems reasonable. The knifer can get help, his neighbours can sleep.

The case, York Crown Paul Tait assures me, "is not over."

Someone should tell Mr. Galanos. He is not home when I visit Graham Crescent, but I phone later.

As far as he's concerned the judge set him free and clear, so long as he stays on his meds and off his victims' property.

"It's over ... it's not even funny how finished it is."

You are right about that, Peter.

"Not criminally responsible means not criminally responsible."

Right again.

He's a self-employed painter and insists he stays with his parents because of legal bills. The attack is clear in his mind, though he's not sure it was a real fishing knife.

"What happened, happened." He tells me he'd apologize to Nicolas and his family if he could only find the words.

Do you think justice has been done, Peter?

"I'm glad to be out, if that's what you're asking."

No, not exactly.

(Note: Peter Galanos was admitted to Whitby Mental Health Centre three weeks later.)

You Were Shot Where?
(January 11, 2007)

Norm Kelly must be trying to sell his house.

How else to explain the city councillor's goofy bid to edit the proud name of our 'hood.

Kelly tells the Sun's Zen Ruryk he wants media to stop using "Scarborough" in crime stories.

No longer will we be murdered, maimed, or mugged in Scarborough. We will be murdered, maimed, or mugged at "Kennedy and Ellesmere," or "McCowan and the 401," or "Markham Road and Eglinton."

Or under that big spruce near the strip mall. Next to the Tim Hortons. Four doors down from the jerk joint. Between the cop shop and the dollar store. A dozen blocks east of Victoria Park Avenue.

Yeah, right there. But, shhhhh, don't call it "Scarborough." Not if it's anything bad.

Believe it or not, Kelly and fellow (forgive me) Scarborough councillor Michael Thompson have presented this half-baked notion to council.

They call it a "media fairness protocol."

It is the reverse of what residents of Jane and Finch demanded of the media years ago.

Stop saying "Jane and Finch" in crime reports. Makes us look bad. Say "North York." Either way, it's a crock. A word trick. Insulting.

C'mon, councillors. We Scarberians are big enough to take the bad with the good.

Just ask our former town crier, Frank Knight, 71. "Scarborough has nothing to be ashamed of and nothing to hide," Frank tells me from his bungalow at Midland and Lawrence, smack dab in the middle of ...

SCARBOROUGH.

"Those councillors are going too far. Let's not be so sensitive."

Bang on, Frank. Too bad you lost your job when amalgamation turned Scarborough from a city of 600,000 into a megahood. If David Miller had sense, he'd make you Toronto's crier. (Knight now freelances.)

Meantime, Mr. Mayor, take this new Scarborough scam out and shoot it. In North York, maybe, or Etobicoke, both of which have crime woes just like us.

Deleting a place name won't change anything. Just confuse people. (Say, hon, where the heck is Plug Hat Road and Beare? There's been a shooting.)

It sure won't cut crime.

Will it raise property values out our way? Fat chance. Maybe if we swap names with Forest Hill we can fool a few people.

But a Scarborough bungalow is a Scarborough bungalow. And "Scarborough is Scarborough," says our ex-crier.

Amen, neighbour Knight. Always has been. We've had crime on our streets since a horse thief made off with an insurgent's nag during the 1837 Rebellion.

That vile steed deed occurred at Gates Tavern, Kingston Road and Bellamy. In ... SCARBOROUGH.

Behind the inn, Gates Gully was a smugglers' lair. Gangbangers first visited us in 1859, with reports of "notoriously bad characters" mugging merchants, farmers, and travellers along Kingston Road.

Littering's a crime, eh? The great Tim Horton once had to apologize to locals for the trash emanating from one of his early coffee shops.

Through it all, for better or worse, we were Scarborough. A township. Then a borough. Then a city. Now a 'hood.

Always a proud name. As lofty as Leaside or Don Mills or Etobicoke or North York or Riverdale or Cabbagetown or Forest Hill or any place where people get shot or stabbed.

True, our collars are mostly blue and our landscape is a tad flat and junky. We have no famous landmark, except the zoo.

"But I don't know why there's this inferiority complex," says Frank. "There's good and bad in everything and we've had our share of glory."

We have given the world the Barenaked Ladies and The Bluffs, Mike Myers and strip malls.

Elizabeth, wife of John Graves Simcoe himself, gave us our name.

Scarborough, after the Yorkshire city, from Skaresborg, named for a malformed Viking chief. Maybe councillors Kelly and Thompson will be happier if we switch to that original name.

Hare Lips' Fort.

OF FAD AND FASHION

Gym Class Is in Session
(April 17, 2009)

As spring arrives downtown, we are all working on our bikini bodies.

In Scarborough, my old 'hood, they never worry about this. In Scarberia, the man — or woman — with the biggest beer belly is automatically elected leader.

Most Scarberians think a StairMaster is some sort of burglar.

It's way different downtown, I'm discovering, as the crocuses and chihuahuas bloom along Queens Quay. Two months ago, I fled the east end and landed in a wee condo at the bottom of York Street.

My building has a snazzy gym, with all manner of machines. You can row, run, climb, pedal, and pump until you are blue in the face.

Through the sweat stinging your eyes, and out the wall-to-wall windows, you can watch other downtowners engaged in jogging, biking, shadow boxing, and other methods of weight loss.

Beach season looms and a wide variety of Quay dwellers are getting ready.

For instance ...

The Groaner. I encountered one of these in the gym yesterday. I thought he was having a heart attack, or multiple orgasms.

"Arrgggruhhh-uh-uh-uh-uh-umph!" he said.

I don't know why. He was lifting 35 pounds. My grandmother could do that without so much as a gentle "umph."

The gutteral gymnastics continued. "Guurrreeeeeesh!" he said on the chin-up bar. "Mmmmmnnnnmphhh!" as he lifted dumbbells. "Urrrrrgpht!" he said, opening the door to leave.

If he snores, it must be awful.

The Poodle Pusher. Cannot walk, jog or run without the aid of a small dog. She (and sometimes he) gets trim in a colour-coordinated way. Usually pink. Her sweatsuit is pink, her headband, her designer sneakers, her socks, her sunglasses, even her poodle is pink.

We have a lot of very fit poodles down here on Queens Quay.

The Sexpot. Gorgeous. Not an ounce of spare fat, except in all the right places. Yet she spends an hour in the gym doing nothing but preen, strut, and distract.

She is found near mirrors and men. I don't know how she stays in such good shape. She must not eat.

The Sweatpot. A different animal entirely. He works up a lather just coming down the elevator.

After 30 seconds on the stationary bike, he's soaked through. So is the machine, and anyone within five feet. Then he forgets to wipe the seat. Yech.

The Barry Bonds. A steroids scandal is just waiting to be exposed at my gym. No way those guys look like that without pharmaceutical help.

Likely, you have several in your gym. In the change room, they are identified by odd rashes and shrunken genitalia.

The Hamster a.k.a Treadmill Hog. Runs and runs and runs. Same speed, hour after hour. Has never heard of interval training, or sharing treadmills.

The Cyclomaniac. Anyone on two wheels, outdoors. Mayor Miller has decreed cyclists are boss hogs in the Big Smoke — and brother do they know it.

They swarm all over Queens Quay. Ignoring traffic signs. Cursing drivers. Scaring barflies and other pedestrians. Surely such surliness counteracts the health benefits of cycling.

Rollerballers. Similar to cyclomaniacs, except they wear inline skates. They are deadly. At least everyone knows how to ride a bike. Few ever master rollerblades.

The Pretender. Akin to the Sexpot, except in looks. Never breaks a sweat, just wanders aimlessly from machine to machine, adjusting, tinkering, staring at levers, and absently scratching himself.

Does he hope to get fit by osmosis?

The Cardio Crooner. She has an earphone full of tunes. And she's damn well going to sing them at the top of her lungs, while trotting on a treadmill.

Her facial expressions are exquisite, like karaoke on crack. Just as annoying is ...

Chatty Chuck. He's not in the gym to work. He's here to network. If he says, "Hey, howzit goin'?" pretend you just tore a muscle and limp away.

The last thing a downtowner needs is to be diverted from his or her springtime imperative:

To look good in a thong by June.

Vintage? Ask a Wino
(June 1, 2008)

Wine critics must go to a special school. Somewhere dry and oaky with a hint of nuttiness.

What the hell are these people talking about?

Our own esteemed wine scribe, Rick VanSickle, refers to a Riesling thusly: "Throws off a note of petrol with citrus and grapefruit backed by bracing acidity."

Petrol? What, $1.20 a litre? Here, have a sip of Sunoco. Whatever you do, don't light a cigar.

The Star's Gord Stimmell describes the "rusty nail notes" of some South African reds, and recommends a California Cabernet Sauvignon with bison sausages. Which is an extremely rare meal at my house.

"A burst of gunpowder presaging a ripe, fruity core," the *Globe*'s Beppi Crosariol gushes about a grand cru.

"Stylish but not demanding," the National Post's Margaret Swaine says of a Valpolicella.

Yes. Nothing worse than a demanding wine.

"Let me breathe! Don't guzzle! Eat your cheese!"

Nor do I wish to drink anything tasting like toast, earth, nettles, crushed stone, tobacco, cedar, smoked game, saddle leather, or tar, all glowing terms used lately by wine critics in the Big Smoke.

I suspect wine snobs are just amusing themselves.

If you plan to tour Niagara vineyards this summer, you'd best learn the lingo. So you appear to know your stuff, though you're just there to get drunk for free.

For instance, if someone says you need a "big, dumb, easy" wine, do not punch him. Big means more alcohol, dumb is a wine so young it still can't "speak," and easy means pleasant.

Wine is fleshy when it tastes fatter than a meaty wine. Got that?

Or it can be peppery, plump, pruney, puckery, perfumed, or ponderous. That's just a few of the *p*s.

Years of study, surely. Or can any Dom, Rich, or Hardy be a wine snob?

Back in the day, I knew wines. Many wines. Quantity over quality. But I'm on the wagon, so must recruit others to a blind taste test.

One bottle is the LCBO's cheapest, a $6 Italian a cut above salad dressing. Another is a saucy little $11 French number. The third is a lovely $25 Aussie Cabernet Sauvignon.

Let's start in the newsroom. Webmistress Irene Thomaidis has a 20-something palate and party eyes. But she picks the Italian salad dressing. "Now, there's a Friday afternoon wine," she beams.

Enjoy, Irene. Pass the croutons. Now, about these other two? Describe them, in wine snobberish.

"Well, if this one is vinegar, that one is piss," she replies.

Maybe this is harder than it looks. I turn to cartoonist Andy Donato, who has swilled more wine than Irene has swallowed water.

Andy picks the Cab right off. But he should know. He makes his own.

Maybe I'll find a truer test where winos live. Can a guy on a park bench match sniffs with a wine snob?

Up to Allan Gardens I go, Sherbourne and Gerrard. Even the squirrels look like they could use a drink.

Six men with paper bags loll under a sugar maple.

"Any of you fellas drink wine?"

Six hands go up. A couple hold bottles of bad sherry.

Pay dirt. Daniel "Frenchie" Roy's mom is a retired sommelier in Rimouski. (A sommelier, you lout, is a wine expert.)

Frenchie, 40, is shorn like a paratrooper, which he was before the chute of life got a little tangled.

"I'm down on my luck right now, but I used to go to art shows and wine tastings. You meet people who don't know what they're talking about."

Frenchie knows how "robe" describes a wine's colour and consistency.

"Though it's hard to tell with a plastic cup, Mike."

And he knows a decent Cab when he tastes one.

Even after a tête-à-tête with Captain Morgan.

"Full bodied, with a touch of fruit and an aftertaste of barrel," he says of the Cab.

Ray Thomson, 53, ran computers and toured wine bars from Paris to Argentina, before IBM downsized him to Seaton House and a regular bench at Allan Gardens.

Ray, too, aces the taste test, though he prefers the little Cotes du Ventoux.

"Not too tangy or pulpy. Sweet, but not too sweet." (Swirl, sniff, swish, sip, pause.) "Perky," he says.

Man, you never know where you'll run into a wine snob.

It's Good, It's Bad, It's Nuts!
(March 24, 2005)

So, pomegranates are the new wonder food. My Dominion

put up a display of the fruit's juice and I have reports of others across the city.

This week the radio said studies show the pomegranate is a super antioxidant, a shield against cancer and heart disease. The 680 News anchor said she's going right home to eat one. Break out the Tahitian noni juice.

Gimme a break.

Maybe the pomegranate will turn out to be God's gift. After all, it is believed to be the "tree of life" in the biblical Eden.

Maybe Eve bit into a pomegranate, not an apple.

But we've been down this road too many times.

They used to say nice things about vitamin E, remember? Super antioxidant. Fountain of youth. Blah, blah.

Now a study shows it does not prevent heart attack, etc. In fact, it can make things worse for some people. Study shows.

You walk into a grocery or a pharmacy and you freeze in fear. Land mines in every aisle.

Coffee. A study finds daily coffee drinkers have half the risk of liver cancer.

But wait! Health Canada says coffee increases bladder cancer in men. And everyone knows it hikes blood pressure. Okay, so switch to ...

Decaf. But wait! Swiss study finds decaffeinated coffee raises your blood pressure, too. Well, the Swiss love smoked ...

Salmon. Ground control to Omega-3. Fatty acids are nutrition stars. Good for arthritis, heart disease, Alzheimer's.

But, wait! Wild salmon good. Farmed salmon bad. (PCBs and other toxins, study says.) Confused? Wait'll you hear salmon farmed in the Pacific is actually Atlantic salmon. Fish farmers and fishermen "lobbing salvoes at each other," says Virginia Zimm, an exec at Faye Clack Communications, which specializes in food marketing.

Well, there's always ...

Tuna. Brain food. Chicken of the sea. But wait! Mercury alert! Don't eat tuna more than once a week. Once a month if you're pregnant or a kiddie.

And for gawd's sake, *make sure it's dolphin-free.* Or become a vegetarian.

Yum ... tofu. As much protein as meat. B vitamins, potassium, zinc. Study says it even reduces hot flashes.

But wait. Study in Hawaii says tofu-eating men are more likely to get Alzheimer's.

Well, at least you can top off your tofu with dark chocolate and a glass of red wine. Both are good for your heart.

But wait! You will be a fat drunk.

Ringing in the ear? I know just the cure ... Gingko biloba. Popular herb. Brain medicine. But wait! Study finds that a placebo fixes that ringing just as well.

Go way back. Cigarettes touted as good for your wind.

And don't get us started on the ups and downs of eggs, milk, wheat germ, carbs, yogourt, beta carotene, artificial sweetener, Atkins, peanut butter, St. John's wort, margarine ...

"It's crazy," says Zimm, 48. "A lot of it is marketing machines at work. Where can we sell our stuff now? Walk into a grocery. You have thousands of choices. Something has to standout and yell, 'hey, pick me, pick me.'"

Right now pomegranate juice is making a racket.

Zimm's brother, Scott Clack, 46, is a Mississauga naturopath. He just read where cheeseburgers make you smart.

"A problem with studies," says Clack, "is they always try for an angle or a spin. It's attention-grabbing."

A study about cheeseburgers making you fat is not sexy.

Unless it's *Super Size Me*, the flick about growing fat on a diet of McDonald's.

But wait! A McDonald's fan struck back. He ate under the golden arches for 50 days and lost 40 pounds. Mind you, he ate only the salads.

"North Americans have a nutritionally challenged perspective on eating," says Clack. "Other cultures have a better balance of protein, carbohydrates and fat."

What about vitamin E, doc?

"The majority of research still favours vitamin E."

Time will tell. There's always something new, rushing to replace the fallen.

Clack is just back from Germany, studying mistletoe's use as a treatment for cancer. The plant is said to combat ills from nervous tension to skin sores.

It also increases your chances of getting smooched.

Kiss My Tattoo
(June 18, 2005)

Once, I told a friend I was thinking of doing something else.

"Naw," he said. "You can't leave that place. You've got the *Sun* tattooed on your ass."

So, when I saw the ad for Toronto Tattoo Expo this weekend, I figured what the hell?

"Which cheek?" asks Kelly Mason, 27, at the Lower East Side Tattoo booth. The right one. It's the *Sun*, after all.

I've chosen the good ol' round logo.

"Not the new one?" wondered Al Parker when I told him the plan. Al is not the big cheese in the newsroom, but he is at least a medium cheddar.

No red square is going on my ass, I told him. Not where the sun don't shine.

So Kelly gets to work. "How long you been doing this?" I ask.

"Since I got out of prison."

Eh?

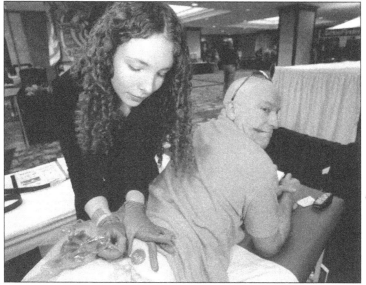

Tattoo artist Kelly Mason leaves her mark, permanently, on Strobel.

Craig Robertson/SUN MEDIA.

"Just kidding."

She started at 17, after high school in Port Perry. She liked making a permanent difference in people's lives.

"Tattoos are a commitment, not like a haircut or something. They're beautiful. You're decorating the temple. It's *life*-changing."

Jeez, Kelly, you're scaring me.

My ass is far from her strangest canvas.

Three years back, she tattooed a doctor's penis, with Japanese symbols meaning love.

He took it like a man, but it is the last penis Kelly will tattoo. "The skin's different and I don't like the, uh, proximity. I'm not going there again."

So, back to my ass.

I check the waiver.

"Are you prone to fainting?" is one of the questions.

Oh, my.

Part of a columnist's job is to inform, to save you the trouble of going out and trying things, like getting a tattoo.

Well, I can tell you that it stings. But not as bad as I thought.

A cross between a sudden sunburn and a mild electric shock. Think of a sewing machine stitching ink into the top layers of your skin.

I can feel Kelly finish the outline.

"Boy, these are tight quarters," she says.

Thanks. I've been working out.

"No, I mean this booth's too small."

Oh.

"How you doing?" she asks. No one has ever actually fainted on her.

Fine. Remember. It's Sun. S-U-N.

Good thing I do not write for the *Halifax Chronicle-Herald*. Oww.

Your rear is sensitive, Kelly tells me, because it hasn't had much exposure to the elements, like your forearm.

Maybe a 5 or 6 on the pain scale. The chest is painful, and the armpits, but everyone is different.

A Discovery Channel crew rushes over. Must be Moon Week, or something. They go off in search of bigger game.

"Welcome to the club," says Dan Adcock, 56. He is up from Lubbock, Texas, for the Expo (a.k.a. the 7th Annual Northern Ink Xposure) at the Holiday Inn on King.

Dan is a landscape. Bears, fish, eagles, snakes, mountains. Every inch is tattooed, except his hands and face.

That way, he can take the honking big ring out of his nose, put on a pin-striped suit and go into Lubbock courtrooms looking like a lawyer, which is what he is.

Kelly has a barcode tattooed on her wrist.

"I was 16. It was very foolish. When you're younger, you don't consider it's going to be there forever."

Gulp.

At 17, she got an alien tattooed on her upper right arm, but she is having that changed into a bunch of lilies.

Otherwise, but for a ring in her gums, she is a blank canvas.

Frankly, she does not look like a tattooist. She says it has become more than a biker-sailor-hooker artform.

Now, it includes that guy over there with the lizard head and the pointy teeth. No biker, sailor, or hooker. Nor a banker, either, I'm guessing.

Kids these days want neck and hand tattoos, like rappers and NBA stars. But Kelly dissuades them. "A big tattoo on your neck limits your career opportunities."

Want a tattoo? Go to a reputable shop. Make sure the artist wears gloves and takes an unused needle out of a sealed package. Make sure equipment is sterilized.

"Ask questions," says Kelly, who also works out of Abstract Tattoo, Queen West. "Use common sense."

Do not get a tattoo of your new girlfriend's name.

Rates are usually $120–$150/hr. Simple designs are in. Art nouveau. Sports logos are common. Newspaper logos? "You're the first," says Kelly.

So, there. I really do have the *Sun* tattooed on my ass.

Of course, they could still fire my ass out the door.

But then I could tell them to kiss their logo goodbye.

When the Fat Lady Sings
(June 17, 2006)

Cera una volta (once upon a time) I went to Italy with a group of other 15-year-olds. When in Rome ... The teachers took us to an opera. The theatre was flowery, gilt-ridden, and cramped.

None of us boys had a clue what was going on, except there was a lot of singing and dying.

So we sneaked out and went to a strip joint. At 15, I didn't fully understand that, either, though I do now. It is like ballet.

Opera remains a complete mystery.

But now we have a shiny new opera house. Everyone says it is the snazziest in the world. You can hear a pin drop. I should hope so. The joint cost $150 million.

Let's learn how to use our new toy.

One evening you may be at University and Queen looking for a bar, take a wrong turn, and land in the middle of *Madama Butterfly.*

In case, you should become a *cognoscente di Opera.* I hope this helps. For starters:

Che cavalo? Perché diavolo non può cantare in inglese?

(Why the hell can't they sing in English?)

Well, say "love." Luv.

Now say, "amore." Ahhhhh-mooooor-ayyyyy.

Gets you right in the gut, eh? Dean Martin was a genius. English is flat, boring, unoperatic.

Want ahhhhh-mooooor-ayyyyy? Go see an Italian opera.

Want war? Wagner's your man. The Germans were always big on war. Wagnerian operas are famous for babes in steel bras and horns, though costumes are less warlike since the Second World War.

"It ain't over 'til the fat lady sings," by the by, has nothing to do with Kate Smith and the Philadelphia Flyers.

In Wagner's five (5!) hour *Götterdämmerung,* it ain't over 'til the soprano brings down the house with a 15-minute solo. (Sans microphone. There are no mics in opera.)

She does not have to be fat, but big lungs are a plus.

"It's not about being overweight," says Ali Kashani, 31, at the Canadian Opera Company. "But chances are opera singers are bigger. Their body is the acoustic of their voice, so a big frame, an open chest cavity, a big throat and a large head help create resonance and a larger sound."

Which, I assume, requires a bigger horse in *Götterdämmerung*. The soprano, all sung out, rides into a fire and dies. The horse dies.

Everybody dies.

After five hours half the audience is VSA (vital signs absent), too.

You might want to start instead with *The Deliverance of Theseus*, which lasts seven minutes, 27 seconds in French, sans intermission.

Ah, the perfect opera. Just as you're dozing off ... it's over!

Now, unless you speak Italian, German, or French, how do you know when to laugh or cry or throw tomatoes?

Normally, you just laugh or cry or throw tomatoes when the guy next to you does.

But the new Four Seasons Centre will thoughtfully scroll translations above the stage. Even for the rare English opera, since you can't understand what they're singing either.

In any language it is easy to tell when someone dies. They bellow for 10 minutes, then keel over.

Tragedy and disasters are opera's stock in trade.

In *La Wally*, for instance, the hero survives being pushed off a mountain, but then dies in an avalanche. His amore, Wally (only in opera could Wally be a she), jumps after him. The audience weeps.

"Operas were the soap operas of their day," says *When The Fat Lady Sings* author David Barber.

"Say, David, ever been to Seville?"

"No, but I used to have a jazz band called David Barber and the Sevilles."

Incidentally, there's also *The Barber of Baghdad*. Nothing to do with Saddam: it is a German comedy.

The Four Seasons will kick off September 12 with Wagner's *Ring Cycle*, 18 hours of power, pomp, and passion. Dwarves, even. And warrior maidens. Frodo would feel at home.

Some helpful hints for when your wife talks you into it?

Jeans are okay. Tickets start at 20 bucks, though you may want to rent a pair of opera glasses.

Or bring sunglasses. Easier to snooze that way. Careful not to snore. The acoustics are incredible.

Try to show up five minutes late. They will not seat you 'til the end of the first act. With opera, that can be two hours.

"Don't worry," says Ali Kashani, "we have beautiful plasma screens in the lobby so you can watch the opera there."

Or switch to the hockey game.

Twin Beacons of Hope for Mankind
(May 14, 2008)

As promised, a column about breasts. You need a good excuse to do this in a family newspaper.

Mine is that I am judging Miss Hooters Canada tomorrow night. (For crying out loud, Mike, another beauty pageant?) Yes, hot on the heels of Miss Universe Canada.

Once you get a rep as an astute assayer of the female form, you can't shake it. So I shall do my duty *vis-à-vis* 20 women from Hooters eateries across Canada.

Oh, the humanity.

But there is more to this than meets the eye. A social trend is afoot.

Breasts, long a victim of political correctness, have bounced back. And they don't mean "bimbo" any more.

Look around. Or on TV.

Brainy Tina Fey has V-necks down to here on her hit *30 Rock*. The best drama on TV, *House*, has breasts as a recurring theme, specifically those belonging to Dr. Lisa Cuddy. Again, no bimbo is she, but the dean of medicine at a big hospital. Dr. House is besotted with her bosom, culminating in a dream sequence strip-tease.

Humour site *cracked.com* this week says CSI forensic scientist Catherine Willows has the top cleavage on TV.

Funny, eh, how real life forensics officers are scrawny guys in glasses. But on TV, billboards, and any street in springtime Toronto, no one is looking at scrawny guys in glasses.

Breasts, of all shapes and sizes, are the bomb, as Randy Jackson would say on *American Idol*.

Even man-breasts. Look at Simon Cowell's. Seacrest can't keep his eyes off 'em.

All of this is healthy. We are emerging from the depths of prudery.

True, recent years have pounded into men the valuable lesson that women are not just sex objects. But, also, a lot of fun was pounded out of life.

Well, life is a pendulum.

At some point, maybe when Janet Jackson ripped her bodice at the 2004 Super Bowl, we scratched our heads and said, "Hey, what's wrong with breasts?"

Next thing, they're popping up all over.

"People are way more relaxed about this stuff, way more laid back," says Miss Hooters International, Breanne Ashley, 23, of Atlanta. Breanne is a fellow judge tomorrow night.

Her tale of the tape says 34C-22-34.

When she hands over her crown in July, she's back to school to become a radiologist.

She tells me: "Anyone who says a big bosom means you're a bimbo, well, they're the ones who are dumb."

Or snobs. Only a snob calls Dolly Parton a bimbo.

In February, Dolly cancelled her U.S. tour because of back injury, saying: "You try wagging these puppies around a while and see if you don't have back problems."

Dolly is a memorable bump on the bosom's trip through history.

Necklines tend to plunge in tumultuous times.

Jane Russell reinvented the brassiere during the Second World War. Jayne Mansfield was two beacons of hope during the Cold War.

Same for Marilyn Monroe and Mamie Van Doren.

Bathing suits even went topless in the unruly '60s.

Breasts hid for much of the '70s and '80s. Rad-feminists and thin-obsessed fashionistas did not like them. Turtlenecks sold like hotcakes. Madonna wore breast armour.

Then, breasts rebounded. *Baywatch* carried us through the recessions and wars of the '90s. A *Baywatch* backlash brought shows like *Frasier*, *Seinfeld*, and *Everybody Loves Raymond*. Funny, sure, but breast-less. *Twin Peaks* doesn't count.

The age of terrorism sparked the current upswing. *Deal Or No Deal*, with its 26 suitcase models, got the ball rolling.

You can argue, as some newsroom cynics do, that breasts never really went out of style. I suppose. As water never goes out of style.

What's different this time?

For one, there's more bosoms, not all of them real.

Breast implants are booming, as public health fears fade, and we all know someone who's got them.

Mostly, I think we're just more comfortable with breasts. Having them, looking at them …

Breasts are no longer so political.

Certainly, any bosom will feel right at home at Miss Hooters Canada.

It's billed as a "delightfully tacky yet unrefined event."

"What you see is what you get," says Breanne Ashley.

I hope I don't go cross-eyed.

Public Privies Are the Pits
(March 19, 2008)

Most of us have mixed emotions about public restrooms.

They are like lovers. You can't live with 'em, you can't live without 'em.

Someone I know never ventures downtown without charting a route past Holt Renfrew.

The pashminas and Prada? No. The *pissoirs*. World-class. A dream.

In Cuba last week, I stumbled into a nightmare. The baseball stadium in Santa Clara, home of the mighty Oranges, has *banos* from hell.

Even my teenage son, usually recoil-less, was pale and shaken after a visit down there. No wonder.

No water. No light. No flush.

No *mas*!

No seats, either, which is standard in Latin America and Asia, outside the big tourist hotels.

In India and China, they don't even bother with bowls, just a hole in the floor. They reckon squatting is au naturel for humans, so why change? Cave men did not have toilet seats. True. They also did not have magazines. Or microwaves.

The weirdest privy I ever used was in the Amazon jungle near a shaman's temple. It was holes in a raised platform. No pit, no door.

Sewage disposal was comprised of ants and beetles.

And giant toads. They wore big pie-eating grins. But what a way to make a living.

Funny how washrooms get into our heads, so to speak. No little hockey fan can forget the communal urinal at Maple Leaf Gardens. Or his first outhouse experience up north.

For something that half a billion people are doing at this very moment, we don't talk about it much.

That's a shame. Offal, even.

So, when I return from Santa Clara, I am happy to see some bumph from *powderroom.ca*. The site is collecting ratings for bathrooms across Canada.

Sure enough, Holt Renfrew has five stars. Union Station so far has but one star. A little harsh, as anyone knows who's been to Penn Station in New York City. There are worse johns in the world than Canada's.

But let's not get too flushed with pride.

My lingering memory of the Pope's sermon at Downsview in 2002 is the portable johns. Unholy.

I once fled a blighted bathroom along Highway 7 because a fair-sized rodent had tired of treading water and had expired in the bowl.

Those are extremes, and you probably have your own horror stories.

But even Tim Hortons restrooms are often less than appetizing. They always smell like burned crullers. I suspect it's intentional, to foil loiterers.

Restaurants, bars, shops, hot dog stands, country fairs, everyone has an inspector breathing down his neck.

So why no toilet police? Why no fines for lockless doors, paperless rolls, yellow bowls?

The mucky-mucks get all misty about accessible buildings. What about people with incontinence?

Well, let's ask an expert. A nurse continence adviser. And I thought those Amazon toads had an odd job.

"Thirty-five years I've been doing this," Fran Stewart, RN tells me from Sunnybrook.

"It's a strange passion, but if you only knew how bladder problems affect women's quality of life."

Powderroom.ca, of which the delightful Ms. Stewart is spokesnurse, caters to women with overactive bladders (OAB).

Men are affected too, of course, though the nearest bush usually works. And there are other incontinence conditions. Not to mention Montezuma's revenge, bad shrimps, and hangovers.

Which gets us back to the gutter.

"Worst I ever saw was in China, in Shanghai," says nurse Stewart. "It was literally just a trough in the ground."

Shudder.

"Our tour guide planned our trips around the bathrooms."

That is *powderroom.ca*'s idea, too. A map of Canada's best, and worst, pit stops. Australia has a National Toilet Map with 14,000 listings.

No one's demanding facilities like the new Japanese models with automatic lids, noise-bafflers, and blood pressure monitors. Just clean 'em and don't let the paper run out.

There's already enough guesswork to bathroom breaks.

On that Amazon trip, a guy named Bill toppled into the river while headed for the loo one inky night.

We were lucky to fish him out. Twenty minutes later he re-emerged from the jungle.

"A lot of trouble for a bit of gas," grumbled Bill.

Yes, and those toads were ticked off, too.

WELCOME TO THE 'HOOD

Oh, Give Me a Home Where the Poodles Roam
(March 6, 2009)

Farewell to ol' Scarberia
Your bluff-bound coast.
Let your strip malls squat and dreary be.
For when I am far away
In the grimy downtown lost
Will you ever flash a thigh

Or fire a gun at me.

So long, Scarborough. I'm moving on up. I mean down. Downtown.

It's not easy. I know Scarberians who have never even been downtown.

Being Scarberian is more than geographic. It is a way of life, a state of consciousness akin to being Buddhist or Jewish or Italian or a Leafs fan or left-handed.

I hate to sound racist, but you can always tell a Scarberian. By his baseball cap, lumberjack shirt, and chipped fingernails. Most of the men are named Bob or Mohammad. The women, Faye or Fatima.

You can smell Scarborough from miles away. Curry. Burgers. Dust. Seagulls. Goose poop. Pizza. Jerk chicken. Marijuana. Gunpowder.

A marvellous, sprawling, brawling place.

But things change in a man's life. Which brings me to a teensy apartment on Queen's Quay and a big dose of culture shock.

Toto, I've a feeling we're not in Scarborough anymore. A few first impressions:

The dogs are different down here. They wear bows in their hair, even the males, and have names like Felicity or Maximillian.

In Scarborough, they're called Hey, Mutt, or Bitch and usually have a touch of rabies.

Downtowners make a bizarre ritual of stooping to scoop up their dog's droppings with a plastic bag. Gross.

Scarberians never stoop that low. Besides, the dog crap hides the litter and rotting leaves.

Downtown is an entirely different climatic zone. It's downright balmy. All those sidewalk grates and skyscraper vents, I guess. Nothing as harsh as the north wind whipping across the savage Scarberian steppes.

The elevation out there also means more snow. Plus, Mayor Miller doesn't really care for anyone in the east end, so there are fewer plows. Or so it seems.

Not that it matters. One of the charms of Scarborough is no one knows how to drive in winter.

Downtown, people drive Smart cars. In Scarborough, they shoot Smart cars on sight.

In Scarborough, pickup trucks rule.

There are more BlackBerrys on one block of Queens Quay alone than there are in all Cliffcrest or Malvern, not counting the ones owned by, ahem, street pharmacists.

So when a downtowner reaches into his pocket, you assume he's got incoming email. If a Scarberian reaches into his pocket, you hit the dirt and pray.

Same thing if you see someone running. In my old 'hood, that spells trouble.

On Queens Quay, everyone runs. They do it in designer tracksuits and Walkmans, or iPods, or whatever they're called nowadays, and they drag a designer dog with them.

Joggers infest my new neighbourhood, even when an arctic gale howls in from Scarberia, past the hookers on Kingston Road and down Lake Shore. Just as Ford F-150s infest the east end.

I look forward to the influx of tourists to the harbour 'hood in a few weeks. I lived in and around Scarborough most of my life, yet I recall meeting only one tourist. He looked scared and confused.

Maybe he was trying to find a restaurant. Fine dining in Scarberia means Swiss Chalet. Which is enough for most of us, but the very thought makes downtown toffs blanch and lose their lunch.

By contrast, my new digs are a stroll from countless eateries offering exotic, leafy, and healthfully meagre meals.

Any self-respecting Scarberian would spit them out in

contempt and light a Players.

Everyone smokes in Scarborough. No one smokes downtown. Tobacco, I mean.

Smoking is just too, yuck, suburban for downtowners. It's way cooler to torture your lungs by jogging in winter.

And there's a lot less booze. Every bar offers non-alcoholic beer. Even the local grocery sells O'Douls. Scarberians just look at you like you're nuts.

So it will be easier staying on the wagon downtown.

Of course, if I see one more poodle in a pink vest out for a jog, I'm gonna need a stiff belt.

Before I hightail it back to Scarborough.

Talk About a Revolution
(January 29, 2003)

The guy in the grey baseball cap takes one look at me and points down the hall.

"The anarchists are meeting in there," he says.

Gee, thanks. Is it the shaved head? Is this anarchist profiling?

I've wandered into a walk-up youth centre on Bathurst Street. One of those beaten-up places that has garish lights and painted brick walls and is always too hot or too cold.

The kind of place where people might discuss revolutions of one stripe or another.

ANARCHIST CAFÉ, says a tiny sign taped to the front door.

Welcome to the Anarchist Free School. Today's topic: "Red" Emma Goldman, a legendary radical who lived a few blocks away at 322 Spadina, over what is now a Vietnamese sandwich shop. She died in 1940.

Now 28 people of like mind sit in a circle to talk about her.

It is pure coincidence I am here the night most of my newsroom colleagues vote to join a union.

Anyway, an anarchists' meeting is quite something.

They don't believe in bosses, government, or leaders. So I get strange looks when I ask, "Are you the organizer?"

There is much discussion about whether I can stay.

The "Shaky Lady" columns I wrote last year, about a bogus bag lady, were not a big hit with this crowd. But everyone has a say and they decide not to boot me. So I get to soak up an hour and a half of anarchism.

These guys have a bit of a bad rep, as you may know. They had their heyday at the turn of the 20th century.

They took a public relations bath when followers murdered the president of France, the empress of Austria, Czar Alexander II of Russia, King Humbert I of Italy, and William McKinley, president of the United States.

Like I said, anarchists have a thing about leaders.

The assassinations "might have been a bit of a mistake," Paul Erato, 48, says dryly. He is an anarchist-gardener.

Germany's vicious Baader-Meinhof Gang also had an anarchist bent. And anarchists have joined other radicals in storming barricades from Seattle to Queen's Park.

"But this is not just about burning down buildings," pipes up a young woman in the circle.

True, my research shows. Mostly. Anarchists are divided. Well, of course they are.

"There are pacifists and there are people in favour of violent revolution," says Dave Fingrut, 29, a bearded bartender.

"I haven't made up my mind yet."

Anarchist/student Valerie Dionne, 26, has dabbled in a bit of good, old-fashioned property damage.

She is a stunner, if you can speak so of an anarchist. Tall, strong, raven-haired.

"I'm a pacifist," she tells me. "But I don't believe destruction of corporate property is wrong because it gets the point across without hurting anyone. And it even creates jobs for people who have to clean up the damage."

Hmmm. And the point you want to get across?

"That we should live a more natural way, with everyone equal and without police or government or laws or taxes."

Oh, yes, I heard about that place. Utopia.

There will be no bosses and everyone can choose their job. So who has to collect the garbage?

Rotate it, says someone in the circle.

No jails, either? What do you do with bank robbers?

Aha! No banks. No money. Of course.

"They'd get a real job," says Mick Black, 27, who's unemployed. "And you'd just go to a store and take what you needed for your family."

I don't think Loblaws would like anarchism.

Funny, though. Emma Goldman, a goddess to anarchists if they allowed goddesses, preached such wild ideas as common-law marriage, birth control, and easy divorce.

And if you listen long enough — less government, no taxes, referenda — they start to sound like the *Sun* editorial board.

Man, they hate Soviet-style commies as much as we do.

There are a few sticky points. Like the end of police, businesses, armies, career incentives ... and life as we know it.

Plus, there's that name. Anarchism. It's derived from the Greek for "without government."

But my *Webster's Thesaurus* lists chaos, confusion, disorder, misrule, lawlessness and riot as synonyms for anarchy.

Hard to imagine voting for an *anarchist*!

But there is no anarchy this night. Just a circle of mostly young people looking to change the world, tilting at windmills, working their minds.

Four of us adjourn around the corner to Sneaky Dee's bar on College. Even early in the week, the joint is hopping. I need to shout into the phone when the anarchists ask me to check on the *Sun* union vote. Waiters sweat. Music blares.

The place is total anarchy.

Getting Naked Before God
(April 17, 2003)

Easter Sunday, Pastor Don Boyd, 51, will rise before the faithful at his gospel church on Bloor Street West. He will preach a sermon called "Brand New Morning."

The congregation will sing #163, Christ the Lord is Risen Today. They will eat hot cross buns.

Easter Sunday, next door at Club Paradise, a leggy blonde named Bunny, 20ish and wearing nothing much, will climb on stage and dance under black lights and a disco ball.

Her music will be more "Highway To Hell" than holy. Men will give her money. Perhaps, though I doubt it, some will be dressed in their Easter Sunday best.

The Lord works in mysterious ways at Bloor and Lansdowne.

This might be the most eclectic corner in Toronto. Sully's Gym, legendary hangout of guys like George Chuvalo, is a rickety climb above an auto shop. Store signs come in a half-dozen languages and as many religions worship nearby.

The Buddhist Association of Canada dominates the northwest corner. Just down from palm- and card-reader Vanessa Demitro, 49, whose front room is full of candles, decks of cards and ceramic Christs.

But the oddest sight is the gospel church, the Bloor

Lansdowne Christian Fellowship, sitting cheek to jowl with Club Paradise.

I find Pastor Don just after a prayer meeting. He is dressed down, with a pen hanging from his neck. He looks and moves like a gym teacher.

His congregation, once called Church of the Crusaders, has occupied this building since 1938. It is a busy warren of rooms. There are evangelists in most of them, planning missions, cooking lunch. A cavernous sanctuary is at back.

A dozen pastors ago, the church tried to buy the building attached to its west wall. They wanted to make it a youth hostel. The price was too steep.

It was a tavern. Always had been. Still is, only now you can get more than a beer.

The doors are, oh, a dozen steps apart and sometimes Club Paradise patrons have entered the wrong one.

So, Pastor Don, what's it like worshipping next door to such sin?

"Visually, it's an interesting juxtaposition of values," he says, a twinkle in his eye.

"But at the same time, what better place to be? Those folks need to connect and hear the good news of Jesus."

Sure, Pastor Don, but 1938. Sixty-five years. They're still there. And now there are strippers.

"We have not done a particularly good job," he says dryly.

It is not for want of gentle trying. From time to time, church members take prayer walks by Club Paradise.

"We pray God will give them a better vision of how to earn an income and free both the guys and the gals from that kind of a lifestyle," says Pastor Don.

A café serving exotic beers would do just fine, he says.

'Til then, UrbanPromise, a ministry sharing church space, has offered to help strippers with babysitting and summer camps for their kids.

No takers, but that's downright neighbourly.

A few months back, the church had a book sale. Two books on bartending went unsold, so someone ran them over to Club Paradise.

Ever, ahem, been in there, Pastor Don?

"Sometimes we get their mail by mistake," he says, a-twinkle. "I just stay focused and look the other way."

"If you're married (he is) then you know what naked women look like."

Well, for one, they look like theeee luuuuuvly Liiiily! She took the stage soon after Club Paradise opened late yesterday afternoon.

Lily is a dark-haired beauty dancing to a Spanish song called "Dance, Dark-Haired Beauty. "

The club's owner finds me at the bar. He's leery. "What are you doing, a 'heaven and hell' kind of thing?" he asked me earlier on the phone. "I don't think God would like that."

But he warms up enough to tell me his name is John. He's 30ish. Church-going Greek Orthodox.

He says he keeps a rein on who gets in. No thugs or falling-down drunks.

"We run a tight ship. There's nothing going on here that shouldn't be going on."

He likes Pastor Don and his flock.

"They're really good neighbours," he says.

"They don't cause any trouble at all."

Welcome to Pariah City
(April 22, 2003)

So, how does it feel? To be the new pariah. To live in Pariah City.

Someone I know calls from Miami. She's helping organize a conference here in May.

"They want to know," she tells me, "is it safe up there?"

You're as likely to be struck by lightning, I tell her, as you are to get SARS.

(Which is not quite true. SARS has taken 14 lives in the GTA this year. Lightning has not.)

But the eyes of the world look warily at us.

This is a new, uncomfortable, feeling.

True, Toronto has had pariah status in the rest of Canada for eons. Because we are big and powerful.

That is not the same feeling as Susan Sarandon and Lisa Marie Presley being afraid to visit us.

The same Susan Sarandon who, in Thelma and Louise, merrily rode a convertible off a cliff. The same Lisa Marie Presley who married Michael Jackson.

And we scare them?

Our civic leaders meet this week about healing what our City Hall Bureau Chief Zen Ruryk calls "the black eye" of SARS.

It will take some doing. Travel the Internet and you will find hit after hit about Toronto and SARS. From America to Indonesia, from Holland to Australia.

Malaysia has banned Canadian tourists. So has Libya.

Yes, Moammar Ghadafi has banned us.

On and on. Slap after slap. Bosox pitcher John Burkett won't sign autographs here. Wal-Mart has barred its employees from travelling here. So have other companies. And do not ask a guy in the tourism business about SARS. He is likely to punch you in the nose.

The convention and visitors association is doing its best.

Its website preaches the low risk of getting SARS. It quotes the tourism minister: "We want to let Americans know they are welcome in Canada and caution everyone against over-reacting." The site is full of cheery reports of people out and about — 50,119 at the Jays opener, 18,000 for Avril Lavigne. The Toronto Wine Show had one of its best crowds.

But I do not think the world is buying it, yet.

If it's any consolation, we are the latest in a long line of pariahs.

Lepers, for instance. They were once made to stand in a grave, with dirt thrown on their heads, in a symbolic death. They then had to wear a bell to warn off other folks. They were confined to huts or asylums and banned from drinking, gambling, playing chess, or having sex with other lepers.

The Black Death. The plague. It was blamed on Lutherans and Jews. For reasons too weird to explain.

The rack, burnings at the stake and other unusual medical practices were used on "carriers."

Mind you, the plague had a silver lining. It introduced quarantine. At Marseille, you had to wait 40 (*quarante*) days to get into the city if you were from an infected area. Say you were arriving at Kuala Lumpur, Malaysia, from Toronto ...

And, in Florence, the first public-health team was formed to combat the plague. A 14th-century version of D'Cunha, Young, Basrur, Low and Co.

Epilepsy. It was believed caused by malignant ghosts. Treatment included exorcism, enemas, castration, and removal of teeth. And isolation.

You would think the stigma would be long gone. But you may have noticed TV commercials are still working on it.

I read that the Flyers held a meeting about SARS before they ventured into Toronto to play the Leafs.

Philly ought to know about being a Pariah City.

Remember Legionnaire's Disease? Philadelphia, 1976. Two hundred members of the American Legion were stricken at a hotel. Thirty-four died. Symptoms were pneumonia-like: Fever, aches, cough, shortness of breath. Sounds familiar, eh?

There was panic, 'til the bug was traced to air-conditioning.

Philadelphia also had more than its share of yellow fever outbreaks in the 18th century.

Other pariahs? Left-handed people. Goes to show how silly the world, and this pariah business, can get. Long ago, lefties were persecuted, killed even, as suspected witches. Joan of Arc likely was a lefty.

Even 50 years ago, parents and teachers were still trying to bind and beat southpaws into correction.

It was so bad, left-handers had 25 percent fewer kids, so their numbers dipped to 3 percent of the populace in Britain, for instance.

But we right-handers came to our senses and the lefty population is flourishing. Look at Mike Weir.

So, being a pariah need not be permanent.

Toronto, there is hope for us yet.

Hit It, Tagalong Paul
(January 6, 2007)

Tagalong Paul has landed in one of his own country songs.

There he is, at a crossroads on the highway of life. Heartbreak waits around the corner. Will he have to kiss his dog goodbye?

The Good Lord keep you, Tagalong Paul.

I find him in Joe's Pastizzi Plus, a regular haunt in Islington. Roadie, his Seeing Eye dog, is at his side. As always. In a corner rests Geri, his trusty six-string, named for a ladyfriend.

Tagalong Paul Stewart, 52, lost his sight to a brain tumour back in New Brunswick when he was six.

If you have ever walked Bloor West Village in the past 15 years, between 10:00 a.m. and 4:00 p.m., you may recognize Tagalong Paul.

A little man with a little guitar, a little coin cup and a big dog.

For a decade, that dog has been Roadie. A big, smart, happy, sloppy, waggy yellow Lab cross.

"Hello, handsome," a woman in an elevator once said.

"Hello, yourself," Paul replied.

"I was talking to the dog," said the woman.

And he has been "Tagalong" ever since.

If it weren't for the dog
I'd have no love at all
I'm just his shadow
I'm Tagalong Paul.

That pooch keeps Paul from walking into walls, growls at petty thieves trying to swipe coins, gets him on and off buses, and keeps passersby covered in yellow hairs.

"Me and that dog," says Tagalong Paul. "It's like a marriage."

Roadie, Paul claims, sometimes covers his ears with his paws on busking duty.

"He figures, 'Man, I've heard that song before.'"

But life is short, especially for a dog. Roadie is 12. That is 64 to you and me. Most guide dogs retire by 10.

Last summer was rough on Roadie, with surgery to fix an infected ear and to remove a growth on his hind leg. The big fella's fine now, but ...

A few weeks back, Tagalong Paul bit his lip and called Roadie's old school in Rhode Island. Was it time for a new dog?

And then some, they said, and mailed the forms.

"But I couldn't do it," Paul tells me. "I called them last week and said I'm just not ready. I can't let him go.

"Maybe if I was in any danger, or if Roadie was suffering in any way. But he still loves to put on his harness and go to work."

When the time comes, a local lady has offered a comfy retirement home, with a nice, fenced backyard.

She helped with the vet bills last summer.

Bloor West Villagers have been good to Tagalong Paul. They bring him coffee and sandwiches, and snacks for Roadie or watch his stuff on bathroom breaks.

I wish they could help him with another bump on the road of life. Writer's block.

Tagalong Paul has put out one CD, *On the Road of Life*, which I keep on my car player between Johnny Cash and Lynyrd Skynryd.

Paul ain't no Waylon Jennings, but his squeaky pitch has some Roy Orbison in it. The tunes are damn catchy, even addictive, often funny, glimpses of his life.

Problem is, the last song he wrote, a tribute to the TTC, was more than two years ago.

Nothing to do with booze. Tagalong Paul has been sober for 15 years next March.

"I'm just coming up empty," Paul says with a sigh. Roadie's huge wet eyes look up at him.

Man and dog rise as one to leave for their apartment, across the street, to watch, or hear, our juniors beat Russia.

Someone gave them a TV. Roadie prefers it to the radio. They are huge international hockey fans, so no busking this day.

Maybe junior gold will inspire Paul to write again.

"Or maybe I could do a new song for my dog."

Hit it, Tagalong Paul:
You never call me darlin'
But you've been a mate to me
You never got drunk or died or ran away
Like those country songs all say
It sure is gonna break my heart
When we have to call it a day.

Barman's Wild Ride
(January 21, 2003)

Sitting in Betty's bar, trying to dream up a column ... The place hums, as usual. It's across King St. from the *Sun*.

"You okay, fellas?" says the waiter, stocky, and close-cropped. We nod. He leaves.

"You'll never guess who that is," says my friend Sam, who spends way too much time in courts.

I dunno, Sam. Jimmy Hoffa? Looks a bit like Robert De Niro.

"Nope. That's the Bicycle Bandit."

And so it is. Or was.

Michael Flaxman, 43. Sharp, articulate, upstanding. New job at Betty's, happy marriage, new house soon. Street rescue volunteer. Nicest guy you'd want to meet.

In 100 days in 1995, he robbed 26 banks. Gave tellers notes that said things like "Give me $500, I'm not f---ing kidding."

He often fled on a stolen bicycle.

A helluva hundred days. With a scary prologue. But a sequel to restore your faith.

My friend Sam knew Michael Flaxman to see him in high school. Sam didn't know Michael was well into a steady diet of booze, cocaine, and heroin.

You've heard, or read, a hundred sordid stories like it.

Flaxman quit after Grade 11, worked tables downtown, and sank deeper in the sewer. Soon he was snorting and injecting two, three grand a week.

He dealt to finance his own habit, but his body craved more and more. It rebelled, horribly, if it wasn't appeased.

"One day," he tells me, "I woke up, had no money, no hopes of making money that day. So I decided to rob a bank."

He wrote a note, donned dark glasses, tucked his ponytail under his cap, and walked into a bank at Yonge and Dundas. It's now a Gap store. He pedalled off with enough to keep the heroin hound at bay a day or two.

And so it went that spring and summer. A couple of tellers told him to buzz off. Which he did, since he carried no gun.

"Sometimes I'd rob a bank at 10 o'clock, the money would be gone on drugs by noon, and I've have to hit another one so I could score again."

He pulled a job every three days, on average.

Then some nice policemen showed up as the Bicycle Bandit stood on his front stoop on Sherbourne St.

They told him he'd left a print at his 17th job. But Flaxman still thinks some other junkie "dropped a dime" on him. Called CrimeStoppers, for the reward.

"Doesn't matter," he says. "I'm grateful. Otherwise I would be dead behind some donut shop with a needle in my arm."

Eighteen hours after his arrest, withdrawal hit hard. Shakes, vomiting, diarrhea. Even his hair hurt.

He was too wretched to realize his climb out of the sewer had begun.

He pleaded guilty to 13 of the heists and got seven years.

Through the thick plastic at Millhaven, he watched his

mother cry.

She had raised him alone, except for a brief later marriage to a cop named Flaxman.

"When she came to see me in prison the first time, it broke my heart. That was the turning point," he says.

But the heroin hound did not go gently. Flaxman found enough dope to give himself an overdose in November 1996.

He crawled into prison rehab. He has been clean since. No drugs. No booze. He works with addicts at the Donwood Institute and is on the board of Anishnawbe Street Patrol.

"There's a part of my past I can't erase," he tells me. "So I might as well make good use of it."

Flaxman got married in June 2000. Shelley, 44, is a feminist-criminologist, with a women's studies degree and a criminology diploma. "I'm her textbook case," Flaxman laughs.

She was an old friend who saw Flaxman's name in the paper and visited him in prison.

"She's my support system," he says. "She's very smart, very beautiful, and I'm the luckiest guy on the planet."

Any guilt, Michael? "No," he says, flatly. "You saddle yourself with the *G* word and you stagnate."

But what about all those bank tellers?

"I think about them quite often," he says, staring out at King Street. "I know I scared them. I'm truly sorry."

The buzz in Betty's rises around us. Flaxman landed here after the old Bamboo club closed three months ago. He worked 16 years at the Bamboo, before and after prison.

He wants to open his own place in a few years.

I would not bet against him.

Fight off the heroin hound, climb from the sewer, and you can do pretty much anything.

They Still Hear "Kid" Play
(February 12, 2003)

The banjo player broke in and found him. He was slumped in a chair, sheet music spread before him. His trumpet was nearby.

In minutes, word got back to Grossman's Tavern: the 35-year musical reign of Kid Bastien was over.

Patrons wailed. Waitresses wept. The Happy Pals left their instruments and milled about, stunned.

Last Saturday afternoon's sun blazed in off Spadina Avenue.

Strange things happened.

Dawn Richardson, 55, put down her tray in shock. She was sure she'd seen Kid walk in. "I was busy, so I didn't pay much attention," she tells me. But about then, banjo man Jack King was searching for his bandleader, who had already missed the first set. Jack busted a window at Kid's Yorkville pad and found him dead of a heart attack at 64.

Christina Louie, 52, whose family owns the tavern, thinks she saw Kid, too. Sitting in his usual chair with the Happy Pals. Her brother swears he heard him singing, though Kid was cold dead by then.

The gritty green walls of Grossman's can play tricks on you.

The place has not changed in decades, except for a coat or two of green paint. Photos of patrons and musicians cover some of the 1960s wallpaper of naked hippie girls.

Cliff "Kid" Bastien's brand of New Orleans jazz bounced off these walls every Saturday since 1968.

His trumpet fairly strutted. His tenor twanged.

One summer afternoon in 1970, when beer was five bucks a case, Noonie Shears walked in.

"Oh my God, that's my music," she told herself.

Soon, she was the Umbrella Lady. She waved a flouncy red brolly and led staff and patrons on a dance among the tables.

Kid's Saturday show always ended that way, as he and the Happy Pals pumped out Bourbon Street.

"He was really something," Noonie, 69, tells me from her usual seat in a back corner. "Best friend I ever had."

Her hair is swept up in a scarf. She has the bearing and lusty laugh of a bayou belle, though she's from New Brunswick.

She and motorcycle mechanic husband John have 12 kids, "about 40" grandchildren and 14 great-grandkids.

It's early in the week. A coupla regulars, chins in their beers. Someone puts on Kid Bastien's CD.

"Kats Got Kittens." "Jambalaya." "Blue and Broken Hearted." Hymns and marches.

It's that catchy, bluesy jazz they played before Louis Armstrong came along. Old, old Dixieland, though Noonie will kill me for calling it that.

"It's New Orleans jazz," she will snort. "New ORLEANS!"

Kid Bastien played clubs in The Big Easy often, sometimes with Noonie and her umbrella in tow. He also played places like London, Ontario, and Barrie.

Jazz doesn't pay. Kid, who was single, also had a sign business.

His birthday was November 21, a day before Noonie's. They always had a jazz party at her house around the corner from Grossman's. He and the band played for her and John's 50th anniversary. Kid was a Christmas regular. Loved her fish cakes and clam chowder.

Each Saturday, Kid took her home in a cab — all three blocks. He always smiled. Never swore. Natty dresser: bow ties and snappy hats. Always tapped his size-7 shoes, even when the music was just in his head.

Kid was born in England, still had the accent. His soul, though, is in The Big Easy. He asked to be buried there.

There was a service Friday at the Unity Church on Eglinton Avenue West. Music started at 1:30.

Kid had the raspy style of namesake Kid Thomas Valentine.

One memorable Saturday, not long before the legendary Valentine died in 1987, the two Kids played Grossman's. It was something. Their trumpets blew the roof off.

Noonie thinks they're up there now, somewhere, tootling through "In the Upper Garden" or "Over the Waves."

The Saturday before last, Kid Bastien and his Happy Pals were on fire. Their gig usually ended at 7:30, but this time they played 'til nine.

"It was like he didn't want to quit," Noonie says. "He played everything, all the marches, it was wonderful."

He closed with "High Society," Noonie's favourite.

He breathed deep, smiled at the 100 or people packed into the place and said, as he always did:

"If the rivers don't rise and God is willing, we'll see you next Saturday."

Well, that was not to be for Kid Bastien.

But every Saturday afternoon, in the timeless, smoky gloom of Grossman's, his Happy Pals will play on.

CANADA, EH?

Our Little Desert Town Perched in the Mountains
(February 3, 2006)

We care so much what Americans think of us. It's pathetic.

When we hear we bore them, we get depressed. Toronto tourism brass report visits from our cousins to the south have dropped 33 percent in five years.

Americans, they say, see only the three *m*s of our land — moose, mountains, and Mounties.

Is this true? Let's take a quickie tour of U.S. tourism icons and ask real Americans.

Where better to start than the Statue of Liberty?

At the ferry terminal, I reach Danelix Ramos, 20.

"What's your take on Toronto, Danelix?"

"Not a clue. Never been there. Don't know where it is. I think it's in the desert. Mountains, maybe."

Okay, let's flee West to San Antonio, Texas. That sacred tourist trap, the Alamo. Two, three million people a year.

Great slogan, too. "Remember The Alamo!" Makes "Toronto Unlimited" look sick.

"Boring?" I ask Alamo executive secretary Laura Garcia, 43.

"Don't know," says Laura. "Don't know anything about Toronto. It's a major city, isn't it?"

"We like to think so. You know it's home to the CN Tower."

"The what? Maybe you just haven't advertised your country or your city enough."

You might be right, Laura.

Up the line we go. Ten metres from the edge of the Grand Canyon, in the lobby of the historic Bright Angel Lodge.

There, Nancy Carpenter, 52, sends mule trains of tourists into the greatest chasm in the tourist business.

"Funny, I don't know anything about Toronto," says Nancy. "When I think of Canada, I think of the wilderness."

Ah, yes, the three *m*s. Not including mules. But you won't find a CN Tower in the bush.

"The what?"

Think of a really tall spruce.

"People say Canadians are dull, but not any of the ones I've met. I mean, there's boring Americans, too."

Next, Mount Rushmore. A tough sled ride from the border. I reach Amanda Holder, 34. She is no South Dakota wallflower. She has been to London, Paris, and Venice.

Toronto?

"I've been to Winnipeg. Is that close?"

"Not unless you're a mosquito. We're on a bigger lake."

"Superior?"

Nope.

"Erie?"

Getting warmer.

"You had the Olympics, right?"

Only in our dreams.

"Martin Short?"

Once in a while.

"Is he Sir Martin Short up there?"

Yes, Lord of Grimley.

"I don't think Canadians are boring," says Amanda. "Sedate, maybe. Reserved." Sure sounds like Winnipeg.

So far, no one has heard of the CN Tower.

Back east, better luck. Lydia Ruth is in charge of the outside lights at the Empire State Building, among other things. She first saw Toronto at 16 and has been up our tower.

"You've got the Eaton Centre and great restaurants."

"Boring?"

"Some Americans when they travel just sit in their hotel rooms, eat fast food, and watch TV, then complain it's boring. They take their boring life from home to somewhere else.

"I love the tower. You can look out and see all those different neighbourhoods."

"I can see it in my mind," says a park ranger at the Washington Monument in D.C.

It is the world's tallest free-standing masonry structure.

The ranger puts me on to Bill Line, 46, spokesman for the National Park Service, and five-time Toronto visitor.

"I think of it as a New York. The most cosmopolitan city in Canada. Great restaurants, theatres. Sophisticated, strong urban environment. A beautiful setting, with the layout and design and feel of it.

"The people there are routinely nice, hospitable, friendly. What's boring about that?"

Sheesh, Bill, we're blushing.

Not that we care what you guys think of us.

Snow Way, Snow How
(December 17, 2005)

So, why is snow white?

Because she just met the seven dwarfs.

No, seriously, what do we really know about snow?

After yesterday, we know it can mess with our minds. Threaten 30 centimetres, give radio anchors apoplexy, then dust us with 10 centimetres.

(680 News refused to cave. Its In-depth Team Coverage! was still shrillin' mid-morning, though the snow was barely ankle-deep and melting in the sun.)

Let it snow, let it snow, let it snow.

Two-thirds of the world has never seen it, except on TV, but it is our nation's marrow.

We should know more about it. Allow me.

So, why is snow white?

It's not. That's an optical illusion. A snowflake's many surfaces reflect light, which our eyes see as white. The flake itself is really a watery grey.

Other things can colour snow.

You know yellow snow, of course. Blue, if you look at it from an angle. There is also an algae that turns snow red.

Those black specks you sometimes see are snowfleas, which forage on dirt mixed in the snow.

Is it true the Inuit have hundreds of words for snow?

No. An urban myth, if you can call frozen tundra urban. Maybe a dozen words, tops, in any of the northern tongues.

The tale seems to have grown from a 1911 report listing four words. That grew with each telling. Sometimes goofily.

One list of 400 words includes *krikaya* (snow mixed with breath), *maxtla* (snow that hides the whole village), and *hahatla* (small packages of snow given as gag gifts).

We southerners have as many words for snow. Slush, flurries, powder, hardpack, mashed potatoes ...

And the most nauseating cliche in the English language. Fluffy White Stuff.

Not to mention hoar.

No, that is not the snow along Jarvis Street. Hoar is a frost formed from flattened crystals.

Snirt? A prairie term for snow mixed with dirt. Black snow.

Speaking of which, Prairie boy John Diefenbaker had a phobia about blizzards. Got caught in one when he was a teen and nearly died huddled in the back of a horse-drawn sleigh.

This federal campaign would have been hell on Dief. No wonder he steered clear of Gander, Newfoundland.

It gets 443 centimetres of snow a year, the most of any town in Canada. Toronto is a wussy 79th, with 122 centimetres.

Oddly, T.O. is more likely to get snow on a Thursday. Just a fluke. (In Winnipeg, it's Monday.)

But we never had a Thursday like the one on February 11, 1999 in Tahtsa Lake, B.C. They got 143 centimetres, the worst one-day dump in Canada.

Tahtsa Lake has not been seen since.

Other fun snow-filled facts:

A large snowflake falls at five kilometres an hour. Snow is 80 percent air. The colder it is, the crunchier the snow. The sound is your boot breaking crystals. And sound travels better in cold air.

So if snow falls in the woods and there's nobody there, does it make a sound?

Dunno. But I can tell you the average life expectancy of a Canadian snow shovel is 2.5 years.

How'd you figure that? I ask David Phillips, my favourite weather man. He is senior climatologist at Environment Canada and the keeper of more weather trivia than is healthy.

"I called around to the snow shovel companies," he says.

"Hey, I've got facts that'll make your hair curl."

For instance, he has calculated how many snowflakes fall in Canada every year. Better sit down.

It's about one septillion flakes.

That's 1,000,000,000,000,000,000,000,000. Volume times square kilometres, or something.

An average snowman contains about 10 billion flakes. That's more than there are in the NDP.

Why our love-hate for snow, David?

"It defines us. We can brag that we're not wimps, that we shun blizzards. And it defines winter. Cold doesn't. The first snow is the real start of winter and the last snow is the end."

So now you are an expert in our national precipitation. Glad I could help.

Come back in a few months. I'll tell you about mud.

Have Storm, Will Travel
(February 7, 2008)

That storm was a wonderful opportunity to observe the many species of winter drivers in our sub-Arctic metropolis.

A new study by *carcarma.com* says your Chinese astrological sign helps determine what you're like behind the wheel.

Rabbits have the fewest accidents and tickets, according to the survey of 100,000 drivers.

"They are better mannered, not in such a rush, and are willing to work with people," says the website's Ashley "Country" Rhodes, a tiger.

Roosters, being cranky, cynical and self-absorbed, have the most accidents and tickets. Rats, whose year this is, ranked sixth of 12 signs. Middle of the road, so to speak.

I'm a goat. An old goat. Born in 1955. So I am a tad gruff and like to butt heads with other drivers, Ms. Rhodes tells me. I don't know about that.

But after my decades of slogging through Toronto winters, a few driver profiles have come into focus. I bet you recognize them all, perhaps in yourself.

For instance...

The Snow Flake. Totally unpredictable. Sometimes he goes fast, sometimes slow. Sometimes he appears to be braking to the beat of a loud CD. Warning signs include garishly painted cars, streamers on aerials, Zen-like vanity plates. Very dangerous. Approach with caution.

The Slush Puppy. Never met a puddle he didn't like. Sworn enemy of pedestrians. Will go out of his way to speed through curb-side pools, then pretend he had no idea.

The South Seas Snail. Drives as though he has never seen snow before, which, in some cases, is quite true. For reasons that mystify the rest of us, he has migrated here from the Caribbean or Australia or Brazil or some such balmy realm. The slightest dusting strikes fear in his heart, and in his right foot. Though glacial in speed, the South Seas Snail is often found in the fast lane.

The Whirly Whiteout. At first, this appears to be a snow devil, a ball of blowing snow. Closer inspection reveals a car inside. The Whirly Whiteout driver, late for work, never bothers to sweep or scrape his car, except for a peephole on the windshield. The only evidence is his nose pressed to the glass.

The Ice Princess. Often at the wheel of a Jag or Benz, she is barely discernible in a mound of fur. Her haughty look matches her driving style. Eyes straight ahead, chin upturned, she imperiously glides through snowbound traffic like a knife through thawed butter.

The Abominable He-Man. Monster of the highway. Young, with sideburns and a John Deere baseball cap. The monster's truck is often black with 33-inch tires and a fog horn. Frightens Smart cars and small Civics.

The Drifter. Moves with skill and confidence, but he is unable to judge where the lines are on snow-covered roads. Lethal, because he sort of sidles into you.

The Spinmeister. Incapable of a light touch on the gas pedal. Spins on every surface known to winter. The good news is, he rarely gets out of his driveway.

Billy the Skid. Hits ice and panics. Often goes straight to Boot Hill. Salvation, says the OPP, is available at *skidcontrolschool.com*.

The Skid Rogue. Related to Billy above, except he slides for show. Why bother turning safely, he figures, when you can spin like the *Dukes of Hazzard*, maybe even do a full U-turn, maybe even into the path of an oncoming semi.

The Phone Squaller. Treacherous in all seasons, but worst now. Gab, gab, gab, brain freeze. For crying out loud, if you can't multi-task, stay off the cellphone unless you're calling in the ski patrol.

The Snow Slow Learner. This species is courtesy of OPP Sgt. Cam Woolley, who tells me of a specimen who spun out on a ramp yesterday. Cops pushed him out. He promptly floored it, smack dab into the back of a transport. The charge is careless driving.

Talk about an endangered species.

Wish List for Uncle Sam
(January 15, 2009)

Lovely to see Barack Obama's White House kissing up to Canada.

We're the new president's first international tour stop. And his rookie secretary of state, Hillary Clinton, says we're tops in her book, too. A "critical" part of U.S. foreign policy, she calls us. I'm so tickled, I'm shivering.

They love us, they really love us.

Funny how much we care, eh? We're the country girl in the come-hither checked shirt, perched at the edge of the dance of the world, hoping the big city boy will say something nice. "Hello, toots," makes us gasp and blush.

Let's forgive Obama for his campaign gaffe about the "president of Canada." Perhaps he saw a President's Choice commercial.

By now he surely knows more trade travels across Windsor's Ambassador Bridge than across the Pacific Ocean between the States and Japan.

So now's our chance. Quick, before they decide they like Botswana better.

The one-way mirror of Canada–U.S. relations, as Margaret Atwood called it, is cracked.

No more "we see you, but you don't see us." And don't get me started on softwood lumber.

As decades of cold shoulders from the south melt away … Uncle Sam, we have a few demands:

First, an obvious one. May we have Florida, please?

It's practically ours already. Some 1.5 million of us come down every year and 300,000 stay the winter.

There's two hockey teams, for crying out loud. Even *Two Solitudes*. The Quebecois decamp on the Atlantic coast, we Anglos on the Gulf.

In exchange, you can have Ottawa. We'll even throw in Winnipeg.

If you won't give us Florida outright, how about a nice tunnel from Harbourfront to Orlando? The Flunnel. Next stop, 30 degrees in the shade.

With your new interest in us, you may have noticed today's forecast high for Toronto is -18. Sit down; I'll explain windchill to you.

Speaking of hockey, we'll trade you some oil and water for the Atlanta Thrashers.

Their last home game seated 10,750. Junior teams around Hamilton and Kitchener draw better than that. Wink, wink.

It's OK, you can keep Gretzky. But not William Shatner. We want him back. Beam him up. We'll trade you another space cadet, Jack Layton. Lock him in a room with Ralph Nader.

Let's talk about Cuba. Hillary's talking all friendly with the Castros, but, you know, we kind of like that embargo.

It means we can wriggle our toes in the sands of Cayo Coco on the cheap without tripping over Ohians or bumping our heads on golden arches or ...

Just a jiff. An urgent request from our prime minister.

He would appreciate it if you would not call him Steve. Or Stevie, Stevie-boy, or Chuckles. Or, "yo, Harper." Says it makes him look too human.

Your last president did that and it pissed off Steve's, excuse me, Stephen's mom.

Also, let's finally declare a winner in the War of 1812. We're tired of hearing how you're waiting for the steroids test results. We won, fair and square. And, come to think of it, you got the White House out of it.

Remember? Our redcoats torched the place and you whitewashed the scorch marks.

Want another war? No? Then keep your seal-skin mitts off our Northwest Passage. Our Inuit found it before your Inuit.

That great Canadian, Roald Amundsen (well, OK, Norwegian) was first to traverse it. So, it's ours. Careful, or we'll call in the frigates.

Anyway, where were you guys when it was nearly impassible with ice?

The Northwest Passage is part of our national identity. How'd you like it if we grabbed the Grand Canyon?

OK? We're best friends? Glad your new brass is paying attention.

Treat us right, and we won't get rough on you.

Jukie's Odyssey Has Surprise Ending
(September 2, 2006)

They shall run and not be weary,
They shall walk and not faint.

— Isaiah 40: Verse 31

Jukie Daly, 29, sits up one day and says, "I am going to walk to Newfoundland."

This is no idle talk. Jukie is the Forrest Gump of Grey County.

You may recall Tom Hanks, as Gump, ran from sea to sea to sea for no particular reason.

Last year Jukie Daly walked from Toronto to Dundalk, 128 clicks, all uphill. After a breather, he walked to Wasaga Beach. All to raise money for a women and youth refuge at his family's Bible camp.

"Where to next year, Jukie?" the Orangeville Banner asked.

Jukie, a construction worker, decided on St. John's, Newfoundland. There, his idol Terry Fox dipped his artificial foot in the Atlantic Ocean 26 years ago.

"Are you kidding, Dean Anthony?" said mom Winsom Dragosits, using his formal name. "Jukie" is dance slang.

Winsom is a Free Methodist pastor and lives at the camp, Destiny's Ranch, just west of Hopeville.

Jukie has a house there, too, with fiancee Angie Garvie, 22.

"No, I'm not kidding," Jukie told his mom, "I am walking to Newfoundland."

So on the Monday of Canada Day weekend, he strapped on his Nikes with soles custom-made by a local chiropractor.

He kissed mom and Angie goodbye, wrapped a Canadian flag over a T-shirt proclaiming his cause, and set off down the camp driveway with his pacer, a teen named Nick.

Nick made it to Orangeville. The hospital patched his blistered feet and sent him home.

"You, too," a nurse advised Jukie.

"No," he replied. "I am walking to Newfoundland."

Freed of Nick, he sped up. All night he walked down Highway 10, turning left at Lake Shore toward Toronto.

Nothing in his kit but a water bottle, a flashlight, and a phone card.

"I decided to rely on God and the kindness of people for food," he tells me.

So he starved all the way to downtown.

One guy thought he was selling flags.

"No, I am walking to Newfoundland to raise money for a shelter."

The guy shrugged and pulled away. No one else gave him any money, either.

The folks at CITY-TV looked at him funny and he went to crash overnight with his dad in Cabbagetown.

"I looked on a map for the fastest way out of town and I found Bloor Street. Then Danforth, Scarborough, Ajax ..."

At some point, he passed near my house off Kingston Road, though I missed him. Would I have given him money? Guess not. No one in Toronto did.

Trenton, Belleville, Kingston, the summer's worst heat wave.

Mostly he stayed in shelters. Some kindly cops in Cornwall put him up in a hotel and got him fed.

Still no money, though. Sheesh, he raised five grand last year. Maybe he needed a big sign instead of just a T-shirt.

Zilch in Quebec, too. He didn't even know how to say "Je marche a Terre-Neuve."

But folks were kind. A sheltermate showed him Montreal and he took in some of the Nuits d'Afrique music festival.

No money, but a man and his kids gave Jukie a half-loaf of bread and three oatmeal cookies. A woman bagged him a baloney sandwich, an orange, and an apple.

One rainy Quebec day, he saw a moose on a hill. A sign he would make it to St. John's? Newfoundland crawls with moose.

He saw or heard other, more menacing, creatures. "Snakes, wolves, foxes, coyotes."

In long, wild stretches of the Gaspe and New Brunswick, fear forced him to bed down in roadside phone booths. At least they were lighted.

"I'm getting really tired," he told Angie from one of them.

"Keep going," she said.

("I'm so proud of him, this man I'm marrying," she tells me at the camp yesterday. They've called me in hopes of post-walk press to keep the shelter plan alive.)

Finally Angie and Winsome get the big phone call, after three weeks and three days.

"I'm in St. John's!" says a delighted Jukie.

But the church woman who was supposed to meet him can't be found. So his family wires air fare.

But first he dips his worn Nikes in the sea, this courageous young man 30 pounds lighter with a heart of pure gold and feet of steel.

As he trudges out of town, headed for the airport, he does not notice the city signs.

Saint John, they read.

New Brunswick.

Make Eh While the Sun Shines
(June 29, 2007)

I always mark Canada Day by watching a Humphrey Bogart movie. *The Maltese Falcon*, for instance.

One of Sydney Greenstreet's hoods snarls at Bogie, as Sam Spade: "Keep on riding me and they're gonna be picking iron out of your liver."

Spade snaps back. "The cheaper the crook, the gaudier the patter, eh?"

Beautiful, Bogie. Make him an honorary Canadian. Jimmy Cagney, too. Up there with Bob and Doug McKenzie. Those guys knew how to play an *eh*.

Do you? A U of T study says denizens of the Big Smoke now use *like* at least 100 times more often than *eh*.

Like, whatever.

Jeez. We're all turning into Paris Hilton.

Our young shun *eh*. Soon only American comedians will use it, when they satirize us.

Stop the slide. Save *Eh* In The GTA. Here is a handy "*Eh* List." Use it as a guide over Canada Day.

Old favourites. Tips from linguists like Elaine Gold of

Queen's, and some uses that might make you scratch your head and say "Eh?"

The Salt and Pepper Eh: The classic. Scholars also call this the "narrative *eh*." Use it like a spice shaker. Whenever, wherever.

"My buddy, eh, went to college, eh, the first guy from around here, eh, and now he's got a CA, eh."

CAA? Battery needs a boost?

"Nope, CA, eh. His car's a-okay, eh, but he can do your taxes in a day, eh."

The Pickup Eh. For the bar before the fireworks start. Pull her nose out of her Moosehead and murmur, "Eh, baby?"

Works well with Canada's other official lingo. As in, "Eh, baby. Voulez?"

The Have Your Eh and Eat It, Too. All-Canadian tongue twisters. "Feelin' good?" "Yeah, eh." "Long day, eh?" Sailors too can play. "Aye, aye, eh!"

The Bossy Eh. "Get your ass over here, EH!" Quick, like a whip. Also works as a one-word order, a version of "Hey!"

The Say Hey Eh! The jock's *eh*. "Willie Mays, what a catch, eh?!" You hear it all over the ACC and Rogers Centre.

"Great save, eh?" "How 'bout those Jays, eh?" Huskier, more manly than a regular *eh*.

The Mocking Eh. This is for use whenever American tourists are in earshot. Loud and proud. Makes 'em giddy, like kids at the zoo. Listen to the cute Canucks.

The Hip-Hop Eh. To counteract the demise of *eh* among our youth. *Eh* is a perfect rap word. Staccato. Easy to rhyme. The rapper Nelly, from Missouri, has broken the ice with:

> *Cause your ass is wack. Your whole label is wack.*
> *And matter fact. Eh eh eh eh eh hear that.*

The Queer Eh. I have met many drag queens, shemales, and others in the "queer culture" wing of the rainbow society. They are the truest of Canadians, adopting a flamboyant, flowing *eh* that does Mae West proud.

The Stand Alone Eh. My favourite. The virgin *eh*. No need to clutter with other words. Just vary the tone to express meanings.

"Eh?" (Sorry, say again.) "Eh!?" (The Leafs traded who?!) "Eh!!!!?????" (Lanny McDonald!!??) Yes, nearly 30 years ago. "Eh?" (I'm old, bitter, and deaf.)

The Yogi Bear Eh. Jovial. "Eh. [Slap on back]. Howzit goin', eh?" Use with caution. Frightens tourists.

The Formal Eh. Smart politicians throw one or two into speeches. Often sounds phony. Like they're slumming.

The Sneering Eh. Drips with venom. Employ at the end of an insulting or sarcastic sentence. "You're a Habs fan, ehhhh?"

Or from Bogart's *The Big Sleep*: "Convenient, the door being open when you didn't have a key, eh?"

The Why Not Eh. Brothers Will and Ian Ferguson, in their hilarious *How to Be a Canadian*, reckon the fathers of Confederation shrugged and said, "I mean, why not, eh?"

How, like, very Canadian.

So, there she be, eh? A guide to our famous, but fading, stereotype. (Actually, it's called a shibboleth.)

Before that "like" slips off your tongue, or "right" or even the dreaded American "huh?" consider *eh*.

It has so many nifty uses.

From Eh to Zed.

Yanks Are Soooo Superior
(October 31, 2007)

*Canadians are a fine tribe of people. They are hardy
— they got to be to live next to us*
— *Will Rogers*

My American friends are incredulous when I tell them their dollar is worth less than ours.

"Huh?" they say, as only Americans can.

Yes, by a nickel, I tell them, for the first time in memory.

Most of my life, our measure as a people has hovered around, oh, 75 cents. That's hell on a national ego. No wonder we have an inferiority complex.

Shrinks get rich off insecurities like ours.

Now that the tables are turned, our next-door neighbours need our sympathy. They need our help.

They need reassurance that their most precious, inalienable right holds true. That they are indeed superior.

In that spirit, my American chums, let's point out a few facts that will make you feel better than us, loonie or no loonie.

Sidney Crosby? You have him. You have Gretzky and Lemieux, too. You also have Daniel Briere, Joe Sakic, Joe Thornton. And most of the Staals. All being paid in U.S. greenbacks.

Canadian NHL teams, except in Alberta, must make do with Swedes for captains.

The War of 1812. You won it, hands down. If you insist. We surrender, already. Sorry about sacking Washington and burning the White House.

You need not curtsy to any queen, except Dolly Parton or Liz Taylor. Your one and true king sang "Don't Be Cruel" better than any of our kings, Edward, George, or William Lyon Mackenzie.

Your footballs are skinnier than ours. Thus, your quarterbacks get a good grip. Your spirals are much tighter and prettier.

You are warmer. You have Hawaii, Florida, California, the Gulf Coast, Vegas, the Valley of the Sun, and Myrtle Beach. We have Pelee Island and the West Edmonton Mall.

You even have more than your share of Virgin Islands. We stupidly turned down the Turks and Caicos when they came begging to be a province.

Your food portions are bigger. Walk into any eatery from Bakersfield to Bangor. You get a plate piled high with mashed potatoes, gravy, and several kinds of meat. Even if all you ordered was the salad.

Our helpings are puny and often hidden under carrot shavings and miscellaneous twigs.

Coincidentally, your lives are shorter than ours, 78 years to 80.3. This could be considered a negative. On the other hand that's 2.3 years less of having to read about Paris Hilton and Britney Spears.

From death to taxes. Yours are much lower, even after yesterday's relief from Ottawa.

Taxmen get 27 percent of your GDP, but 37 percent of ours. To you, GST is a sports car.

Your beer is way more versatile. Use it for anything that requires water.

You can wash your car with it, rinse your mouth, or even soak your plants. But if we pour a Brador, or even a Moosehead, on our philodendron, it's dead in five minutes.

You have lower gasoline prices. We are puzzled by this, since we have more gasoline. Then it dawns on us. Taxes, again.

You are better workers. I read where a Canadian is only 82 percent as productive as an American.

This may be related to the strength of our beer.

David Hasselhoff. You and the Germans know a fine singer when you see one. Best we can do is Celine Dion, Shania Twain, Michael Bublé, and Diana Krall.

You are blissfully unaware of us, which is a Godsend to both countries. It means Rick Mercer can do shows like *Talking to Americans* and have them say "I are sorry to hear Nanook of the North has been traded to Nashville." It means you don't even have to know when we're poking fun.

Best of all, you take a lot of crap from the bad guys of the world. A tonne of it. So we don't have to, so much.

At the very least, neighbour, that's worth a dollar or two. Canadian.

Keep the change.

GOOD SPORTS, BAD SPORTS

Habs Fans Can Bite Me
(April 16, 2008)

Oh, man, I hate Habs fans.

One of them, Alice Newton, reminds me why.

She, among others, is upset by a line in my column last week about how our descendants will look when Toronto's ethnic groups meld.

The only taboo, I suggested, was mixed marriages

between Leafs and Canadiens fans.

"Who the heck wants their kid to look like a Habs fan?" I wondered.

Well, go ask Alice.

"Utterly assenine (sic)," she writes. And that's one of her kinder comments. She vows to tell Quebecor CEO Pierre Karl Peladeau.

"Shame on you!!!" she says. (To me, not PKP, who I believe is actually a Leafs fan, too.)

"Were you insinuating that Habs fans are inferior to others?"

Well, no, Alice, but come to think of it …

Here's a few reasons Habs fans get my goat.

First, they are too damn touchy.

Then there's Boom Boom Geoffrion. What kind of fans, outside a strip joint, call their stars Boom Boom? Or the Rocket. Or the Pocket Rocket. Or The Flower. Or Big Bird. Or St. Patrick.

Or Gump.

Leafs fans never do that. We just add "er" or "y" to everyone's name. As in Caber, Steener, Matt-y, Arm-y, Ponikarovsky.

Montreal fans are hung up on the letter *H*.

They have puffed this up to be the biggest little letter in sports, resting famously in the big *C* of the team logo.

Think it stands for *Habitants? Mais, non!*

Likely "Habs" started as a mistake by Tex Rickard, owner of Madison Square Garden, in 1924.

Somehow Tex connected *les habitants'* meaning Quebec farmers, with the *H*.

A nickname was born.

The *H* actually stands for hockey, as in *Le Club de Hockey Canadien.*

Well, we know it doesn't stand for humble.

Habs fans are arrogant, and often cruel. They tell Leafs jokes, such as: "What do Habs fans have that Leafs fans don't?"

"Colour photos of the Stanley Cup."

Tres amusants.

When they aren't telling silly jokes, Habs fans subscribe to the Principle of Divine Right. The Liberal Party does, too. Liberals believe they are God's chosen government. Same thing for followers of the New York Yankees.

Habs fans? The chosen ones?

Well, it is true the Yankees' 26 World Series wins only recently surpassed Montreal's 24 Stanley Cups as the watermark of franchise success.

It is true the Habs passed the Leafs in that category before I was born.

It is true Montreal has won 10 Cups since the Leafs' last in 1967.

But this is pure luck, not divine right.

Even when they lose, they're lucky. The Habs missed the playoffs last year, a glorious chance for Leafs fans to gloat. But we missed, too, damn the luck.

This makes their rags-to-riches turn this year all the more galling.

Speaking of divine right, Habs fans have forgotten the Sermon on the Mount. "Blessed are the merciful."

They boo at the drop of a hat. Zdeno Chara, just because he's tall. Darcy Tucker, because he's from Toronto. The American anthem. The other team's stickboy.

Not only are they rude, they're everywhere. I have seen Canadiens sweaters from Stonehenge to the Amazon.

Even this newsroom is infested with them.

Copy editors, who only come out at night, are especially susceptible. And underhanded. Im afrayd theyy wil git evven by mesing wit ths colunm.

Sometimes, as deadline nears, you can hear them surreptitiously humming, "Ole, Ole, Ole."

This is the Habs fan anthem, and one of the lamest in sports. Not to mention, they stole it from European soccer.

Indeed "ole" means thief in Nigeria. I do not know how they say "arrogant" in Nigeria.

Habs fans try to tell you they are "confident," not arrogant. But they say it with a smirk.

Leafs fans never smirk. In fact, we don't smile much at all.

Ooooooh, man, I hate Habs fans.

Cannonball? Run!
(August 14, 2008)

I wash my hands of cannonball diving. This once proud and thunderous sport has become, well, what's the word?

Silly.

The tide turns at Summerville Pool, Woodbine Avenue and Lake Shore. The Trident Splash National Cannonball Championship.

I'm so proud to be a judge again, I interrupt my vacation for the day. Who the hell needs the Olympics, anyway? Let Steve Simmons write about that.

I bet Steve has never been a cannonball judge. I bet he sneers at the very thought.

Maybe he has a point.

A black wall of cloud menaces from the west. What a summer. Behind us the grey lake glowers.

The low point comes in Round 3.

Lawrence Stockwood Devansky III, 28, of Toronto, climbs to the five-metre platform. Devansky III (and I don't think that's his real name) performed an earlier jump dressed as a banana.

This time, he peels down to a thong that would make Britney Spears blush.

Sheesh. And cannonballers pine for the Olympics.

In the stands, tots turn enquiring eyes to their moms.

A seagull squawks and banks away.

There is no card for "0," so I give Mr. Devansky a "1." But the mood is set.

For an hour, we watch grown men leap as chickens, as a pussycat, in a giant blue cowboy hat, as a bumblebee, a butterball turkey, a pony, with pompoms …

What is this, a sport or a freak show?

Then, a beam of reason breaks through the clouds.

Brian Utley. The Hurtin' Albertan. Former cannonball champeeeen of the world.

In 1981, he took the torch from the water-logged, wrinkly hands of world champ Butts Giraud.

Yes, that Butts Giraud. He once cannonballed into a tank of killer whales.

Utley came out of retirement to claim the national crown last summer. I was there. My toes still tingle.

What a triumph it was for true, uncontaminated cannonballing. The pure, divine displacement of water with maximum force that inspired its German name: Arschbombe.

This year, Utley, a Calgary teacher, is here to defend — before retiring.

"The Last Splash," he calls it.

Even Brian has gussied up his act, though. An entourage leads him onto the pool deck of battle, handing out Canadian flags or Hawaiian leis, lumbering along to the Beach Boys, or the theme from Rocky.

But when Brian, 55, drags his carcass on rickety knees up those 16 stairs and stands before us, his soul is bared. No wigs or wings. No thong, praise be to Jesus.

Just the integrity of the tuck.

"I let my splash speak for itself," he always tells me. Clint Eastwood could not put it better. If Clint weighed 388 pounds.

Brian's splash and a spritz of nostalgia get him into the final.

And it's close, 55 to 54 from us six judges.

But Doug Bergmann, 29, a 305-pounder from Edmonton, wins in a clown's wig and a dress to the beat of a can-can.

For this, he gets $2,000 and a year's supply of Trident gum.

Bergmann's leap is not without heroism. He cracked his foot while practising in Lake Erie two days ago. Plus, he must pause mid-routine while Devansky III retrieves his thong from the pool bottom. (Don't ask.)

Doug, runner-up last year, is clearly the crowd favourite. That's modern-day cannonballing for you.

A perfect tuck means squat, nowadays. It's all about the frills. Still, Bergmann is gracious in victory.

"Brian's awesome," he says. "The dominator of our sport. I feel bad if I stole his glory, this being his last year."

"I'll respect the position and I'll do it honour."

His clown wig drips on my notebook.

Utley?

"I'm very disappointed," says Brian, mighty shoulders sagging. "I thought I made a bigger splash, but that's not what it's all about, I guess."

So, champ, time to splash off into the sunset?

"No. I think I'll be back next year."

Oh, oh. The Brett Favre of the five-metre board.

I wonder if the New York Jets need a cannonballer.

Let's See. Which Spell is Which?
(September 22, 2007)

This ought to do the trick, soccer fans.

"Zeus, Lord of Olympus," Tamarra James cries out. "Receive this offering of precious incense and turn your eyes to this place."

A cloud crosses the midday sun over BMO Field. A gull keens. A security guard shifts nervously.

Ms. James, 56, is high priestess of the Wiccan Church of Canada. She is this country's top witch.

We are here, with her deputy witch, Nicole Cooper, 31, to put a spell on Toronto FC.

A good spell. A spell to bring a harvest of goals. Or at least one. Starting today, with Columbus in town.

As any suffering FC fan knows, the team has not scored in nine games. Not once. No even on their own net. Not even in practice, I hear.

In desperation, I have called Tamarra. "Sure," she says. "Can you pick us up?" What, no brooms?

So I zip over to Tamarra's place off St. Clair Avenue West. She is wed to high priest Richard James. They own the Occult Shop on Vaughan Road.

Their house must drive kids wild on Halloween.

"What are you going to dress up as, Tamarra?"

"I guess I'll be a witch."

Even at noon on a Friday, my spine tingles.

Careful, don't bump the table guarding the Sleepy Hollow driveway. Finely carved African black granite, it is dedicated to Hecate, goddess of witchcraft.

A gnarly old oak crowds the front yard. Halfway up, a mask of Zeus gazes out at his realm. Indeed, he peers directly toward BMO Field. Zeus is chief god of the heavens, and of sports.

The first Olympics were in his honour.

Witches Tamarra James and Nicole Cooper, background, end nine-game scoring drought for Toronto FC soccer club.

The entrance to the house is darkest gumwood. Eerie eyes peer from picture frames. A room brims with books on potions and black notions. Wands of wood, clay and crystal. Egyptian myrrh. Ethiopian jawi. Coconut resin. Amazon copal. Hemlock gum. ("Not the poisonous one.")

Sandalwood. Sulphur.

On the second storey, a few steps below the temple, is an altar to Zeus. In bronze, he wields his trademark lightning bolt.

"He's the god we'll be working with," says Tamarra.

(I hope we haven't blessed the game with a thunderstorm.)

Beneath the bronze is a softball, signed by a prison team. The Jameses do outreach rituals for Wiccan convicts.

Now, to business. Hi ho, Hi ho, off to BMO we go.

Team officials won't let us on the field. Oh, toil and trouble. So Tamarra and Nicole set up at Gate 3. Close enough for Zeus, Lord of Sport.

They have brought their best frankincense. Five bucks a bottle back at the shop. Plus a goblet of wine in homage. A nice full-bodied Australian shiraz.

Tamarra holds it to the heavens. Sweet frankincense sparks on a stand of charcoal. She calls to Zeus:

"Hear me as I ask your blessings on this stadium, where bold men will strive on the morrow to wrest victory in the field. May their efforts delight your eyes. Let their battle be glorious, yet grant safety to these men in their exertions.

"And (this is the biggie), let those who behold the contest see many goals over which to raise their voices in wild cheers of approval."

The cloud drifts off the sun. The dying light of summer bathes red bleachers where goal-starved fans will sit today. A flag ripples. The high priestess lights a Viscount.

"Nothing in life is guaranteed," she says. "But I have a deep and abiding belief in Zeus. To me, sport is a link to antiquity, a gift from Zeus. We've invited him to watch this game." Just to be sure, I dust Gate 3 with something another witch gave me years ago: Jinx Removing Powder.

"Think of a dark cloud hanging over the team," Tamarra directs. "Then picture you removing it."

Done. So, if you are going to today's game, keep an eye out for Zeus. You will know he's about if TFC breaks the drought. Or if it rains and thunders. If either happens, thank my good witches.

Okay, ladies, let's talk about the Leafs.

(Abracadabra, it worked. Toronto FC scored early in its next game.)

In the Mauler's Corner
(June 8, 2008)

"I hate this," grumbles Sasha "The Mauler" Mrvic, 21, posing for photos.

"I know, Mauler, I know. You'd rather be whuppin' some ass. But this is part of the 'ultimate fighting' game. Trust me. I'm your press agent."

Freckles flicker on her *Anne of Green Gables* nose. Her pigtails twitch.

We're at Twin Dragon, St. Clair near Dufferin, where The Mauler trains.

She glares at me.

"Hey, what's with this 'Mauler' crap?"

"As your press agent, Sasha, I advise you to have a nickname. All great fighters have one.

"Iron Mike Tyson, Bonecrusher Smith, Smokin' Joe Frazier, Sugar Ray Leonard, Tommy 'The Hitman' Hearns."

"Marvelous Mrvic?" she asks drily.

"Marvin Hagler already took that, Sasha, though, pound for pound, I think you're more dangerous."

Sasha "The Masher" Mrvic, might work, but it's a tongue-twister. The ring announcer will implode.

(Mrvic. Say Mer-vitch.)

"Your dad called you Tank, right? When you were five and beating everyone in judo."

"Yeah. Boy, oh, boy. Whatever happened to ballet?"

"And that's a Sherman tank tattooed on your calf, right?"

"How'd you know it was a Sherman?"

"A hunch. I think General George Patton would have liked you, Sasha."

"But 'Sherman' Mrvic sounds like a rabbi. And 'Tank' Mrvic could be a football lineman."

"Anyway, let me worry about it. I'm your press agent. You concentrate on beating the snot out of other girls."

Her grey eyes gleam.

"Just give me two minutes with 'em," says The Mauler, with wistful menace.

She climbs through the ropes to practise on boyfriend Devin.

On June 19, Sasha, a middleweight, will stalk another foe, at Paradise Banquet Centre in Vaughan.

Mixed martial arts, a.k.a. ultimate fighting, is banned in Ontario. So officially this will be a demo bout, part of a kickboxing card.

As her press agent, I will be in her corner, literally, with Alfie Dellaterza, 43, her trainer of six years.

If I get blood on me, I doubt it will be Sasha's.

That *Green Gables* nose is pristine, never broken, though the same cannot be said for her opponents. She has won 11 straight MMA bouts, most in the States, and busted half a dozen schnozzes in the process.

Her only loss was to American judo pro Stephanie

Mariscal before 3,000 fans in Chicago in 2004.

Sasha broke Mariscals nose and orbital bone, and popped out her shoulder. But Stephanie, that wily vet, surprised her with a rear naked choke hold to win.

"The bitch," growls Sasha. "Or is that too negative?"

"Leave it to me. I'm your press agent. Which reminds me. We need ring entrance music."

"Usually, they play rap. I mean, do I look like a rapper?" says The Mauler.

I'll see if I can rustle up the theme to *Rocky*.

That's what she plays in her earphones during 40 hours a week of hills, situps, pushups and sparring. She never preps for a specific foe. In fact, she prefers not to even know who she's about to slaughter until she steps in the ring.

No game plan. No holds barred. Sic 'em, Sasha.

"A light switch goes on in her," says Alfie.

One time, she was toying with someone. Fed up, Alfie went over to help coach the other girl.

"Sasha freaked, put her on the ground, threw a few shots and ended it right there."

The Mauler's roots are judo, but her arsenal includes Shotokan karate, pankration, Goshin jiu-jitsu, and kickboxing.

Plus, a bewitching smile.

"Which reminds me, Mauler, we need a slogan. Like Muhammad Ali had 'float like a butterfly, sting like a bee.'"

"You think of something. You're the press agent."

"Right. Try these: 'Look like a fashion model, fight like a man.' Or, 'Excuse me, I need to powder your nose.' Or, 'Call me sweetie-pie, I'll call you an ambulance.'"

But she's already gone off to beat on Devin some more.

"She's gonna be world champion," says Alfie. "I can even see her fighting men."

"I'm telling you, Mike, we've got something special here."

A press agent's dream.

Goalies Are the Loneliest Heroes
(April 15, 2004)

The great Jacques Plante once shook his head and asked: "How would you like it if you were sitting in your office and you made one little mistake? Suddenly, a big red light went on and 18,000 people jumped up and started screaming at you, calling you a bum and throwing garbage at you. That's what it's like when you play goal in the NHL."

Sometimes.

Eddie Belfour has been called a bum a time or two. Not lately. In the first two games of the Ottawa series, The Eagle was Mr. Zero, before the dam burst last night.

His eyes blazed through the gap in his mask even during O Canada. Nothing's getting by, boys, they said. Other end of the ice, Patrick Lalime was doing his Zen thing, bobbing his head, eyes glassy.

Goalies are an odd lot.

Do not say "Hiya, Ed!" to Belfour before the game, lest you want a goalie stick upside your head.

Glenn Hall puked before every game, then went out and invented the butterfly style. His teammates wanted his bucket in the Hall of Fame.

Gump Worsley used to say the only worse job was javelin catcher at a track meet.

You know how, growing up, the goalie was always the weird kid? I know a guy named Kevin who has a ceremonial beer before he minds net in his Pickering men's league. No self-respecting winger would do that.

Punch Imlach called Johnny Bower the world's best athlete. But Johnny, a.k.a. The China Wall, a.k.a. The Snake, was always hazy about his age.

His published birth date says he was 42 when he helped the Leafs win their last Stanley Cup, and is 79 now.

"Naw," says our dapper George Gross. "He's got to be 85."

On the phone, Johnny cackles. "I think George started the whole thing about my age. He must have the wrong stats?"

Johnny takes a break from mopping the floors at his Mississauga home to explain what makes netminders tick.

"It's all desire, but it starts when you're a kid. Nobody wants to play goal, so someone says, 'You try it,' and the next thing you know, you're a goaltender."

"I never played forward a day in my life. I'd have got killed out there."

"So you put your mug, no mask, in the way of cannons like The Rocket and Beliveau, and Howe?"

"Yeah, like being target practice for Joe Louis."

Bower had 37 career shutouts, plus five in the playoffs. So he knows the roll Ed Belfour was on against the Sens.

"It starts to get to them. They've probably looked at all the films, trying to figure out how people have scored on him."

Bower knows that a hot goaler is one flinch away from goathood.

"You're only human. And there's nothing behind you but the goalposts."

Down the QEW, in Fort Erie, Ed Chadwick, 70, is tuning up his golf clubs. He knows a thing or two about streaks, hot and cold, and the fickle fortunes of a netminder.

He tended goal for the Leafs in the late '50s, bounced around the AHL, and scouted until a couple of years back.

The Leafs called him up from Winnipeg in '56. Ninety seconds into his first game, against the mighty Habs, Boom Boom Geoffrion blew one by him.

"Oh oh," thought Easy Ed. "Back to Winnipeg."

But in the next five games, to season's end, he was undefeated, with two shutouts and a scintillating .60 GAA.

"I couldn't even remember how I stopped all those shots," he tells me. "Sometimes, everything works."

At the other end, of course, another goalie was being a bum.

As Frank "Ulcers" McCool, of the 1940s Leafs, put it: "The goalie? If he blows one (everyone) knows it. Pretty soon, the goalie feels like an outcast. The only friend he has is the other goalie across the ice.

"He's the only one who understands."

Where Are You, Bill Barilko?
(April 16, 2004)

Our heroes, often, are shooting stars. A flash in time. A moment of brilliance.

Paul Henderson. Terry Fox. Greg Joy. Laura Secord.

Bill Barilko.

The Leafs have a new rally slogan. BB16. Bill Barilko, 16 wins to the Cup.

Most young fans know of Barilko only from the Tragically Hip tune. "The last goal he ever scored won the Leafs the cup ..." You've heard it a million times. The words are framed in the Leafs' dressing room.

Here's a taste of the story behind them.

April 21, 1951. Saturday. Crisp and cloudy. The official forecast, an odd omen: "Rain, followed by showers."

At the Uptown, *Abbott and Costello Meet the Invisible Man*.

A few blocks away, at Maple Leaf Gardens: Game 5, Stanley Cup final against Montreal. Toronto leads series 3–1, all overtime games.

Overtime again. Barilko, 24, has a busted nose and penalties for charging and roughing to show for regulation play.

"When you ran into Bill Barilko," teammate Howie Meeker tells me from B.C., "it was like running into an anvil. Any part of him could hurt you."

Two minutes into OT, forwards Meeker, Harry Watson, and Cal Gardner are pressing. Meeker, all hustle, has the puck by the end boards to the right of rookie goalie Gerry McNeil.

Says Meeker: "That goddamn, great big (Habs defender) Tom Johnson comes from the other side and puts me face-first into the glass."

Meeker scoops the puck out front and, angry, turns on Johnson, stick ready.

"You big son-ovabitch ..."

Suddenly, magically, the red light glows.

Harry Watson, to McNeil's left, has taken a whack and the puck has caromed toward Barilko at the faceoff circle.

Did you see the goal, Howie? "Hell, no, my face was in the glass."

Barilko dives. Swinging his stick in a sort of backhand, he goes top left. McNeil is still down. He tries to swing his blocker across, but it is too late.

Funny thing, Barilko was caught pinching up in an earlier game. Cost a goal. Leafs' exec Hap Day warned: "Stay back, Billy, or you'll end up on the farm club in Pittsburgh."

"But he kept on pinching," says Meeker. "He had a good sense when to move up. Like that night ..."

Barilko is airborne, stretched above the ice, suspended forever. Immortal, though in the last months of his life.

"I shook Tom Johnson's hand," says Meeker, "and we've been friends ever since."

As Howie turns up ice, Barilko is already hoisted in triumph by defencemates Garth Boesch and Cal Gardner.

Meeker, a new and historic assist to his name, rushes up, beams at the grinning, toothy kid and ruffles his mop of curls. "Great shot, big guy," he says.

Referee Bill Chadwick fishes out the puck and tosses it to Jimmy Main, in his wheelchair next to the goal judge.

"Here, Jimmy, take this home to your mother," grins Chadwick.

In the Leafs' dressing room, Barilko's mom, Fay, down from Timmins, ladles champagne from the Stanley Cup. The toothy grin has not left her son's face.

"He was always happy," says Howie Meeker. "Always up. He was a born hockey player and he'd be in the Hall of Fame if he'd lived.

"He was having the time of his life."

Howie and a pile of other Leafs were lounging at Shopsy's at the Ex that summer, when they heard Bill's floatplane was missing up North.

"We knew we'd lost a big part of our defence. And a big piece of our heart."

Bill Barilko, we sure could use you now.

The CFL. Nice Guys Finish Last
(October 20, 2006)

The Argos are this city's guilt trip.

They have given us moments as cherished in local sports lore as any Maple Leaf, Blue Jay, Rock, or Raptor.

Never has our town housed classier warriors than Pinball Clemons and Damon Allen and John Avery. Yet we neglect them. Turn up our noses. Tune out. Leave them in the hands of a few rabid fans.

Mea culpa. Here I am at the press launch for Grey Cup Festival 2007, and I cannot remember the last time I went to an Argos game.

I suspect many of you are in the same boat, men.

What a shame. We owe them better. There is much riding on next year's festival and Cup game.

We last hosted in 1992. You are forgiven if you do not recall.

What a dud. The city yawned. There wasn't even a measly parade. Prime Minister Mulroney skipped the game.

So did most of us, unless you were a Blue Bomber or Stampeder fan (Calgary won).

Scalpers were unloading $125 seats for 15 bucks.

Maybe we were miffed the CFL at the time was wooing franchisees in places like Sacramento and Albuquerque. Maybe we were just smitten with the world champion Jays.

Whatever, they moved the big game out of town and it has stayed there, lo these 15 years, in cities that appreciated it, like Regina, Edmonton, Winnipeg.

Shameful, really, when you consider 45 Cups have been played here, including the first. In 1909. U of T beat Parkdale Canoe Club 26–6.

In 1909 we were not a world-class city with world-class sports. We were Regina.

We did not have $55-million pitchers, $43-million power forwards, or Swedish hockey players making $7 million a year.

We did not dream NFL dreams.

Average CFL pay now is about $50 grand. For the season. Hardly world-class, eh? The NFL minimum is $275,000, though you have to play an extra down.

Not likely an NFL team would pull a guy from a sales meeting at work to replace their injured kicker.

Charming, maybe. Folksy, working-man cute.

This must be why Hogtown mostly scoffs at the Boatmen and the CFL. They are bargain bin, therefore not worthy.

You will be stunned to hear the CFL once paid on par with the NFL. Even before million-dollar babies like Rocket Ismail.

Ask your kid how the Argos are doing this year. I doubt he even knows they are in first place in the East, at 10–6.

That they have won eight of their past nine in a gutsy comeback the Leafs must envy. That they can clinch against Saskatchewan tonight and Montreal next week. That they are the gritty kind of team that won the Grey Cup in 2004.

Likely, your kid will stare at you blankly.

This, though there are no better ambassadors to our young than the Argos. They are in schools more often than many students.

In the field of goodwill, petit Pinball Clemons alone is worth the weight of the Jays' infield.

A CFLer comes cheap. So does a ticket. An end-zone "red" at Rogers Centre costs $160. For one season.

Same price as a red for the Leafs at the ACC. For one game.

Yet the Argos never come near a sellout, drawing slightly less than 30,000 including packages and giveaways.

Surely Grey Cup 2007 will be different, especially with the Argos so resurgent on the field.

A one-day cross-Canada sale through Ticketmaster ends at 4 p.m. today. Next chance is in March.

Most of us world-class-city dwellers will tune into the Grey Cup, as usual. It is our Day of Atonement to the Argos for shunning them the rest of the year.

It never used to be that way. I remember where I was when Leon McQuay slipped and fumbled in the rain in Vancouver to cost us the 1971 Cup.

I remember huddling with classmates Monday mornings, dissecting games and trading cards.

I remember meeting Garney Henley like it was yesterday. Garney who?

A gentleman, but he played a fast, open game. Entertaining. Like the Grey Cup, usually. Or any regular Argos game, so I hear.

And Henley was pure, unassuming class. Meet Damon Allen and you will know what I mean.

I don't know that the CFL has changed so much. Our city sure has, though.

We've got too world-class for our britches.

We don't know what we're missing.

I think I'd better get to a game.

Watch the Stickwork, Jiri
(Nov, 16, 2007)

Maple Leafs rookie Jiri Tlusty has learned a priceless lesson: Keep your head up around the Net.

Jiri, 19, sent cellphone photos of his naked self to a few close friends and Holy Mackinaw! they landed on websites.

The phrase "keep your stick on the ice" has new meaning.

"It will not happen again," Tlusty's statement promised.

But it could happen to any of us. You can't be too careful these days.

Some tips on how not to wind up nude on the Internet:

Don't Be Stupid. This would seem to pretty much cover it, but human nature is not built that way. So ...

If She Yells "Cut" After Making Love, Check the Curtains. And, whatever you do, don't bed Pamela Anderson. Motley Crue's Tommy Lee and Poison frontman Bret Michaels have starred with her in different Web flicks.

Pam is becoming her own genre, especially since marrying Rick Salomon a month ago. Salomon was the "unwary" Paris Hilton's sex-romp co-star.

Kid Rock, another ex-paramour of Pamela's, stars with Creed's Scott Stapp and groupies in a video. Rock calls Stapp an idiot for losing the tape. The Naked and the Dumb?

Practise What You Preach. Dr. Laura touted such values as premarital celibacy to her 18 million radio listeners. This got tricky after nude photos of her surfaced on websites.

Ms. Schlessinger was in her 20s when she posed for a beau. She had yet to write *How Could You Do That?* or *Ten Stupid Things Women Do to Mess Up Their Lives*. Her fickle ex-lover was near 80 when he leaked the photos. Goes to show there is no statute of limitations on nude photos. In case you were hoping.

Stay Out of Politics Unless Your Closet Is Bare. Last week, Oz was abuzz about Family First Party star candidate Andrew Quah, 22, now dubbed "Australia's Smallest" politician on various websites.

"That's not my p----," he insisted, though he admits he might have been drunk and posed for some of the pics.

"Look, maybe somebody Photoshopped it," said Quah, a pianist. "I can tell you it's not me."

Moot point. End of campaign.

The mayor of Albion, New York, Mike Hadick, this summer weathered his own nude photos being posted online, arguing they too were doctored. His Honour also faces a drunk-driving rap and last week his daughter was busted for selling cocaine.

Never Enter a Beauty Pageant. We've come a long way, baby, since Miss USA 1957 quit because someone squealed she was a married mother of two. Now, posting naughty photos is the preferred way to de-throne a queen.

Vanessa Williams, Miss America 1984, recovered nicely. Time will tell about Miss Great Britain 2006 or Miss Nevada 2007 or Miss USA 2006 or Miss Teen USA 2006 or ...

Be The 300-Pound, Tattooed Wife of a Police Chief. Surely, that guarantees your birthday suit never sees the light of day.

Unless you post them yourself, as Doris Ozmun did last year.

"My wife is 6-foot-3 and weighs 300 pounds," Snyder, Oklahoma, Police Chief Tod Ozmun told reporters, after resigning.

"If there is somebody that thinks they can control her, have at it. I have tried for 11 years and haven't been able to."

Don't Drink and Drive. Booze is a common theme in Internet nudity. But the cops who pull you over? Houston officers stopped a tipsy college student in 2005, somehow got hold of her cellphone and downloaded the nude photos she'd stored therein. Soon the photos were making the rounds at the precinct.

Reduce, Reuse, Recycle. A garbageman chanced upon nude photos tossed out by Marcia Cross. *The Desperate Housewives* star "looks absolutely fabulous," said an agent hired by the garbageman, not fabulous news for Ms. Cross.

If You Work for Walt's Company, Shower Fully Clothed. Nude photos of Vanessa Hudgens, 18, star of Disney Channel's *High School Musical*, magically appeared on the Net in September. Somewhere, Walt shuddered.

"We hope she's learned a valuable lesson," tsk-tsked a company rep.

Let It Ride, It's the Least of Your Worries. The New York press reports O.J. Simpson starred in an Internet video with two women. The Juice admits he appears, but claims an impostor later staged the sex scenes. If the glove fits, you must acquit?

And young Jiri Tlusty thinks he has problems.

SEXUAL PREFERENCES

Swinging's Their Thing
(February 6, 2008)

We should all pile in the family wagon and see what the heck is going on down in Viagra, I mean Niagara, Falls.

The Cheese Capital of Canada never fails to amaze.

Where else in the world can you imagine a daredevil in a barrel surviving the plunge only to drown in a heart-shaped bathtub?

Where else are wax figures and whack-a-moles the biggest ethnic groups?

Where else could an army of swingers, and I don't mean Tarzan, take over a major hotel and convention centre?

Charles Blondin, meet Sexyboots. Both acrobats, but in different ways.

Blondin walked a tightrope across the Falls. Sexyboots, well, she just walks a tightrope.

"There's a fine line between love and lust," she tells me down the line from her home in Barrie. "I can love my husband, but lust after someone else."

And vice versa.

Sexyboots is not her real name.

"We're where gays were 50 years ago, when if you admitted it, your career and family and social life were ruined." So, Sexyboots it is. Let me guess.

"It'd be obvious if you saw me in a club," she says. "I have a large collection of 'hooker boots.'"

I hope the carpets at a certain Niagara Falls hotel are up to the challenge.

Two hundred couples will convene for a Valentine's Day weekend called Take a Bite of the Apple (TABOTA).

This is not for the faint of heart.

The exact location is hush-hush. (I'm sworn to secrecy. But it's not Motel Sex ... um, Six.)

And single men are *not* welcome.

"It may seem like a double standard," says Sexyboots, 37, "but we find single men far too pushy. A lot of couples don't like that. They feel pressured.

"There's also the 'creep' factor. They're single for a reason."

By the by, don't call it "wife swapping" or risk a face slapping.

"Swinging" is still okay, but "the Lifestyle" and "lifestyler" are preferred. Rita DeMontis will be tickled, I'm sure.

The bumph from TABOTA organizers says this is the first hotel "takeover" by swingers in Canada.

A Super Bowl of group sex, with teams from the many clubs that dot Ontario, even bedroom communities like Barrie.

"A whole hotel works better," says Sexyboots. "Otherwise you might have a floor of swingers next to a floor of peewee hockey players.

"What I do in my bedroom is my business, but I have no right to expose my lifestyle to others. We won't be making out in the halls."

Mind you, the promo does promise "a hedonistic and sexually charged atmosphere."

Seminars include erotic photography and tantric sex. The pool parties, speed-dating, and theme dances sound like fun. So do the group sex and bondage rooms. Gives "smoking floor" a whole new meaning.

Sexyboots will be there with her hubby, a computer guy who goes by Mr. Boots.

They were college sweethearts and have two kids. She works for Queen's Park.

Five years ago, after he'd been hinting for months, she said, "Let's do it," and they went to a swingers' Halloween party dressed in army fatigues.

"Isn't this adultery, Sexyboots?"

"My definition of cheating is doing it behind your spouse's back. But I'm not. He's right there with me."

"Playing," swingers call it. As in: "Listen, I'll play with Buffy over there, you play with Lars and Sven, and later we'll play 'Simon Says' with Bob and Carol and Ted and Alice, play a little Flying Burrito Brothers on the hi-fi and if we have any energy left, maybe play some Scrabble."

As the promo says: "What do committed couples do to relieve the seven-year itch? Scratch it together!!"

"Wha...?!" says Niagara Falls Mayor Ted Salci, just back from a chili cook-off.

Your honour, that's a real swingin' town you got down there.

"This is the first I've heard of it." He laughs. "They're local people!?"

From all over. The hotel's not exactly broadcasting it.

"If they're law-abiding, I suppose it's fine."

Even in a God-fearing place like the Falls?

"Well, I won't be cutting any ribbons for them."

Too bad, Mr. Mayor. There goes the swing vote.

If You Go Down to the Woods Today ...
(July 30, 2008)

God must love swingers. Or He has just given up on them.

Either way, the rain stops in time for body-painting.

Hail passes to the south, mercifully. Nothing puts a dent in a swingers' picnic like hailstones on bare skin.

One kilometre across Stoco Lake lazes unsuspecting Tweed. Big muskies lurk beneath those grey ripples.

I hope the swingers know that, because the men skinny-dipping are dangling the right bait.

A few locals claim Elvis lives incognito in Tweed.

The King sure could swing, but I see no sign of him at the Teddy Bare Picnic.

I do find my pal Sexyboots, of Barrie, Mr. Boots and their very dear friends Mr. and Mrs. Sexxxmaniac. (What is that, Latvian?)

If you go down to the woods today
You're sure of a big surprise ...

166

Tweed, population 1,540, is no shrinking violet. It elected Canada's first all-female council and once tried to lure a CFL franchise.

Alas, the Tweed Muskies got away.

But the village also has nine churches, which presumably consider wife swapping a sin.

"I've been playing dumb," says Casey Trudeau, 25, who owns Trudeau Park, site of the swingers' picnic and tent city.

"Corporate campers," Casey tells townsfolk.

> *Ev'ry teddy bear who's been good*
> *Is sure of a treat today*
> *There's lots of marvelous things to eat*
> *And wonderful games to play*

I will sum up the official program, most of three days, as delicately as I can: meet-and-greet, bikini dance, bonfires, body painting, wet T-shirt contest, bands including Bobnoxious, oil wrestling, naked girl bowling, foam pit.

Foam pit? You betcha. You never know who you'll meet in a room full of bubbles.

What, no weenie roast?

The big draw, though, is the unofficial activity. The sort that has Casey fearing for his pool table.

"They moved the balls and cues out of the way and went at 'er," he tells me.

The "play room" off the dance floor in the lodge is stocked with mints, hand sanitizer, lube, condoms.

Must I paint a picture?

Casey and mate Cheri, 24, learn a lot over three days with 200 swingers, though they must already have had an inkling, since she's expecting in November.

They learn, as I did, that not all swingers swing alike.

Bed-notchers are predatory couples with one thing in mind. **Unicorns** are single babes, the queen bees of any swingers' picnic. **Wallies** are the ants: single lads, like the ones from town who cruised by on a pontoon boat, looking for action or trouble or both. Security chased them off. You can tell the **newbies** by the blushing.

I find Theresa Davis and Jeremy Nash, 20-somethings, in their tent tucked close to the park exit.

Theresa wears a collar that says BITCH, though she is anything but.

"We figured on throwing some spice into our lives," she tells me.

Her tattoo says, in Chinese, "Never regret." Easier said than done. Swinging goes both ways.

"I don't want another man," she says, gazing upon Jeremy. "And, I mean, last night, a woman came up and grabbed his ass. I didn't know what to do. We're still kind of on the fence about this."

Safer than being on the pool table, I guess.

Theresa and Jeremy had to return to their tent four times the first night, just to calm down. I wonder if they'll be at the August bash on Lake Erie.

Another thing I learned: Swingers are always "going for a nap."

I meet Jeremy Visser and Sue Cutler, both 28, who are not swingers per se. But he was the ninth caller to a radio station and won two $140 passes.

They are just back from a nap in their tent. They went to bed early the night before.

"We were really tired," says Sue. "And we wanted to be asleep before it got too noisy."

Yes. All that snoring.

Anyway, have fun, kids. Sunset nears and I don't want to turn into a pumpkin. Or any other kind of gourd.

"Not staying for naked girl bowling?" someone asks.

No thanks. Pool is more my game.

Sugar, Spice, and Duct Tape
(June 3, 2002)

Lola Rodriguez pulls an itsy-bitsy, beige bikini from the pile of clothes on her kitchen table.

It's for the swimwear event of the first Miss Shemale World Pageant.

Blushing, I blurt out the obvious. "Shemales have male genitalia, right? How are you gonna hide it in that bikini?"

Lola rummages through the pile.

"This," she says, triumphantly. It's a roll of duct tape.

"No kidding?" I say, wincing. "Can't wait to tell Red Green."

"Hurts a lot when you pull it off," says Lola, 34. Her Venezuelan accent is strong. She's been in Toronto two years.

She's lived as a woman for 10 years and has had about as many surgeries. She has breast implants — 40D. She had two ribs removed for the hourglass look — a 28-inch waist. Her forehead has been lifted. Nose narrowed. Lips plumped. Cheeks chiselled.

A few hours before last night's pageant, Lola wears a Modafest pin-stripe pant suit, sheer top, red wig, and soft-bronze lipstick. She's 5 foot 10, 130 pounds.

Her pitbull, Puppy, ducks in and out of the semi near Jarvis and Carlton Streets. She keeps him in line with a spray bottle.

She has worked as flamenco dancer, hat saleslady, and ship cleaner. She wants to open a bed and breakfast for gays and shemales.

"I'm not kinky, just a little revolutionary," Lola says.

She sometimes walks topless along downtown streets. She has drawn startled looks at the nude beach on Hanlan's Point. And then there's the pageant at El Convento Rico, a nightclub on College Street.

It is billed as "Bringing it to the Mainstream." As far as organizer, hostess and shemale Amanda Taylor knows, it's a world first.

I'm not sure how eager the mainstream is to embrace this kind of thing. But Labatt, Stella Artois, and Smirnoff are sponsors. CITY-TV maestro Moses Znaimer is a judge.

"I don't know if we were ready to do this before now," Amanda tells me. "We wanted to do it in the mainstream. Gay people already know about us. We need to teach the mainstream."

Well, there's a lot to learn.

Like, which washroom does a shemale use? (Ladies.)

Then, one of the dumbest questions I've ever asked anyone: "Is Amanda Taylor the name you were born with?"

"I was a boy, silly," she says.

"Oh, right. Sorry."

"It's okay, honey, I live in suburbia. I get questions like that all the time. I understand we're different, that this is new for most people. That's why we're doing (the pageant). So gentlemen like yourself can be educated about us."

Amanda is a standup comic and web mistress. She says she's 35ish.

She says shemales are a "third gender," content to keep their male equipment, but go feminine everywhere else. And live as women. Always. Unlike drag queens.

"Ever, you know, surprised the hell out of a date?"

"I would hope none of us goes to bars, pretends to be a complete woman and picks up men."

I reckon a lot of men share that hope, Amanda.

"If a man ends up in a relationship with us," she says, "he already knows what he's getting into."

Amanda thinks there are "a couple thousand" shemales in the GTA. Apparently, only six have the cojones to enter the pageant.

"We put the word out on the Internet and we hoped it would be international," Amanda says. But her trip in from Mississauga is longer than that of any of the contestants.

"Just baby steps," she says. "I think the world's shemale community is watching to see what happens."

Pageant hour draws near, Lola shows me the Guzzo wedding dress she'll model in the fashion event, with a female friend in a groom's tuxedo. Sheesh. The Miss CHIN bikini contest is never this confusing.

Welcome to the shemale world. And, lo and behold, Lola is its queen.

Crowned at midnight last night. Her swimsuit routine is a smash. The wedding dress bit bowls 'em over. She wins the pageant, with its $3,000 prize. "I'm so proud," Lola says.

"Hey, here we are," Amanda tells me. "We can have fun like anyone else. We want you to understand us a little bit."

I dunno, Amanda, Lola.

I'm already having nightmares about duct tape.

Out with Mike, in with Michelle
(June 22, 2006)

Paddy Aldridge sees me frown and she switches my rack of 38s for a 40DD.

"Everybody wants bigger tits," she sighs.

We are in her Take a Walk on the Wild Side shop on

Strobel channels Jennifer Aniston.

Gerrard Street East. Upstairs is her private club for cross-dressers.

There, she helps lawyers, country singers, farmers, truck drivers, all sorts of fellers, "transform" for a night on the town.

I am here in honour of Pride Week.

Goodbye, Mike. Hello, Michelle!

Paddy tells me skimpy is back in fashion in the gender-bending world. You will notice this at Sunday's big parade.

"Global warming is having an effect. Halter tops with revealing backs are in. Baggy is out. Hot pants and short-shorts are in style again."

Not for me they're not. Got anything in a burka?

"Look at this beautiful flesh-tone lace," coos Paddy, 51, holding up one of Wild Side's panty designs. "It will be like you have nothing on."

Perhaps I will wear it on my head.

And forget that Wildside Jayne Belt thingie.

"Converts a Tarzan into a Jane," says the bumph.

Sorry, I like my bumphs just the way they are. I will give it to the neighbourhood kids to use as a slingshot.

Listen, Paddy, can we move on to the stockings?

"Beige!" she calls out to her assistant Julie, a.k.a. John.

Then she inspects the hair on my legs.

"Make that black!"

They are bow-tie lace. Gorgeous. Naughty, but not slutty. The shoes are size 11, with four-and-a-half-inch heels.

How the hell do dames walk around all day in these things?

"Chest out, shoulders back," barks Paddy. She finishes my makeup.

Boys, did you know they actually glue on those batting eyelashes? Same for fingernails. Mine are strawberry, with cute little flowers at the tips.

"Don't they make you feel feminine?" says Paddy.

Yep, and it's real easy to scratch yourself.

My lipstick is Red Alert.

What to wear, what to wear. What would look good with $220 40DDs?

When Paddy opened Take A Walk On The Wild Side 20 years ago, she had a couple of wigs and her getups from her days as Miss Fancy Free, star of joints like Starvin' Marvin's.

"You came out looking like a stripper whether you liked it or not."

Now, well ... your wife could go nuts in here.

How 'bout that little fuchsia French maid number? I'll walk across to Allan Gardens and scare the winos. Not to mention my 16-year-old son, Jackson, who is going to hop the first freight train to Tuscaloosa when he sees this.

So, no French maid.

"It's just not you," says Paddy, and she dives into the rack.

Out comes a sleek, crushed-velvet dream. Queen size, I am sorry to hear. And that's with a corset on tight as a mouse's arse.

Paddy, by the by, is a howl, with a somewhat confusing sexual history. Fresh off the strip club circuit, she married a transsexual woman named Veronica. Married? Yes. They were able to prove Veronica, father of one, had XY chromosomes.

Later, Paddy married a cross-dressing trucker named Roxy but they, too, divorced.

Most cross-dressers are straight, she says. Or bi.

It's a hobby, like stamp collecting. Sort of.

Julie/John, an IT guy, was married 20 years.

"I used to throw on jeans, T-shirt, and work boots and sit there and wonder why my wife was taking so long to dress."

Now, he is resplendent in Capri pants and loop earrings.

"Any fashion tips, Julie, especially with these damn shoes?"

"It's like skiing. First time, you're going to fall 80 times."

I'm already up to four when Paddy starts tossing wigs.

Photographer Mark O'Neill likes me in the Marilyn Monroe, which worries me. But we settle on Jennifer Aniston.

You can see the resemblance in the photographs.

Any minute now, I am expecting a call from Brad Pitt.

"Come back to me, Jen."

Buzz off, cad, I will reply.

I'm way too much woman for you.

Another Reason to Say "Oh, God!"
(October 19, 2007)

The Bible has some pretty steamy scenes. A lot of begettin' going on.

But no pictures.

And for sure nothing like you will find at this weekend's Everything to do with Sex Show at the CNE grounds.

God is everywhere, though, and His presence is strongest at Booth 1527.

JESUS LOVES PORN STARS, the banner says.

There, churchgoers will hand out free Bibles. The Automotive Building houses many sinners this weekend, so they have brought 2,500 Bibles and expect them to go fast.

Maybe they will even outdraw the chocolate penises in the next stall.

The House of the Lord has come to the sex show. Actually, two houses. The Discovery Church, of Bowmanville, is the local ally of American porn-fighter *XXXChurch.com*.

The latter is making its first foray into Canada.

Co-founder Mike Foster says God spoke to him in the shower five years ago.

"Triple X," He said.

Ever since, XXXChurch has held Porn and Pancakes breakfasts and set up shop at sex trade shows. Members distribute groovy little Bibles inscribed "Jesus Loves Porn

Stars" and ask if anyone wants to walk a purer path. They are careful not to preach to the perverted.

"We are not here to bring down the porn industry," says Discovery's Peter Kooger, 32, unloading Bibles at the booth. "We're like AA is to alcoholism. We're here for anyone who wants to get out of it."

When the show opens later today, Peter will roam outside the building, praying his brethren inside are not overwhelmed by what they see.

Good luck with that, Peter. Every kind of dildo, whip, lube, harness, chain, stiletto, swing, ring, thong, dong, dungeon, bustier, and blowup doll will be on display. It is amazing what you can strap on these days.

The congregation will love the fake orgasm contest.

"I find that I am walking with my eyes on the carpet," says Pastor Martin Spoelstra, 41.

"If I could snap my fingers and make this go away, I would. But the reality is, it won't. But I also believe God has hope for the people here as much as anywhere."

Amen. The porn people even kind of like these guys.

"We were really skeptical at first," says show spokesman Mikey Singer, 28. "Were they going to make trouble?

"But the people at other shows said the XXXChurch people were fine. And their Bibles are kind of cute.

"I don't agree with their message, though. Someone was arrested in Texas for selling a vibrator in a lingerie shop.

"We don't want to go back to the 50s when sex was considered a bad thing."

The XXXChurch's pink, yellow, and blue Porn Mobile is headed to T.O. from home base in Michigan when I reach spokesman Brandon Piety, 22.

"That your real name?"

"Yessir. Legally."

XXXChurch's list of the saved-from-porn includes such

stars as Sierra Sinn and filmmaker Donny Pauling.

"Some people say, 'Oh, you're getting too close to porn by going to the shows,'" says Piety. "It was shocking at first. But then you see through it all, through the glam. They're just people doing their thing. We'll help if they want help. It's what we're called to do."

Here comes a likely candidate, in heels and a sailor suit.

Maxine X, 32, is Canada's Top Fetish Porn Star. Her stock in trade includes bondage and some things I can't mention. Her 41 videos include *Asian Heat*, *Stocking Stuffers*, and *Sex Addicts*. Latest is *Asian Pantyhose II*. A crew from Showcase is tailing her for the reality show *Webdreams*.

"At first I thought it was a joke," she says of the strange flock setting up at Booth 1527.

"It's risky for them, because we're taboo, us porn people. But at the same time they're being positive. We all think so."

"So, you believe their slogan about Jesus?"

"Actually, I'm Jewish."

Oh.

Moses Loves Porn Stars.

Floggers Work Out the Kinks
(February 6, 2003)

Toronto's S&M crowd is on pins and needles. A superstar to that set, Fetish Diva Midori, wings in today from San Francisco.

Hide your belts and wooden rulers.

Over four days, she will teach three classes at Queen Street West adult store Come As You Are. Japanese rope bondage. Feminine dominance, Level 1. Aural sex. Aural, not oral.

On Saturday, she will teach Flogging 101 at Northbound Leather, a sort of leather Mecca on Yonge at Wellesley.

Northbound's kinky stuff is at the back. A frigid wind blows me in off St. Nicholas Street, a lane behind the store.

To my left is a rack of scrotum harnesses. To my right, the tear-drop shaped weights you can attach to them.

I wince, gird my loins, venture deeper into a leathery world.

Two staffers agree to talk about Midori and their world of BDSM. As in bondage, discipline, sado-masochism.

In their community, they are known as Boy Wynter and Vita. So, let's call them that.

Boy Wynter, 25, is from Edmonton. He is slim, soft-spoken. Vita, 22, could play a cousin in *The Addams Family*. Eye-catching in cherry lips, lime eyelids, and blood-red hair. Sharp, too. She's in linguistic anthropology at U of T.

She also is in charge of dress code at the door of Northbound's monthly fetish parties.

You can't wear jeans, except under leather chaps, or expose any nasty bits. Not if you want to get past Vita to use the spanking benches or suspension devices.

"I've read that nine out of 10 people have engaged in some form of S&M," Vita tells me. "Anything from a bit of blindfolding to wrought-iron shackles and a dungeon set up in the basement."

I ask the obvious question: "Doesn't it hurt?"

"Maybe someone who's getting flogged for the first time would say, well, yes, that hurts," she says. "But someone who's conditioned can feel the subtleties and knows there's more to it."

Adds Boy Wynter: "They would never describe it as pain. They would say 'that stings,' but never, 'that hurts.'"

Behind the cash is a wall of whips and floggers. "If you're not experienced, get a well-balanced implement," says Boy. "Or you'll tire out or your marksmanship will be poor."

A good starter goes for $150. A purple Spanish calf suede number runs $219.

On a budget? A genital flogger is just $25.

"So who's into this stuff?"

"A lot of people you'd never guess," says Vita.

Well, I've wondered about my banker. He's always cracking the whip.

Maybe he goes to "munches," informal, non-sexual gatherings of BDSMers over lunch. They may talk about masochism or about the Maple Leafs. Same thing, really.

Or he may go to the club fetish nights popping up around town. Northbound's annual blowout at The Docks draws 3,000 people.

Sounds like BDSM is becoming mainstream quicker than you can say Marquis de Sade.

Fashion's a factor, of course. Look at runway shows. Look at movies. Hell, look at your kids' clothes.

And Vita thinks it might be related to the fad of body modification — piercings, tattoos and the like.

Whatever, Diva Midori is riding the wave. She is 36, 5-foot-2, born in Japan. Corset waist, 18 inches. She is, perhaps, the only former U.S. army reserve lieutenant and former pro dominatrix. (Shine my boots, soldier!) She wrote *The Seductive Art of Japanese Bondage* and teaches classes and couples.

Last time in Toronto she tutored a lawyer and her TV exec hubby. I beg her to tell me who. Really beg. No dice.

I've reached her in San Francisco. Any Flogging 101 tips, Midori?

"Get the right tool for the job," she says. If you want a nice, velvety flogging, get a nice, velvety flogger.

Oh, and be careful of eyes and kidneys.

Learn where your partner stores his/her stress so you can flog it out of him/her.

And, floggers, be wary of repetitive strain injury. Especially if you type for a living.

How'd you get into this, Midori? She sounds surprised.
"Well, gosh, I like kinky sex."

Okay. Isn't there a danger of getting carried away? Of really hurting someone?

"Naw, it's like spicy food. People get to the point where it's more than they like, then they back off."

So there you have it, from the fetish diva herself.

I would love to visit one of her classes this weekend.

But I'm all tied up.

Bent Outta Shape
(May 12, 2005)

We may never know for sure if Dr. Tony DeLuco's penis is dogleg left or dogleg right.

Or, as he says, "straight as an arrow."

We are on tenterhooks yesterday at DeLuco's discipline hearing before the College of Physicians and Surgeons of Ontario. A penis expert is expected to report on two studies he made of the beleaguered member's member.

But defence lawyer David Humphrey rises to say he will not call urologist Dr. Ara Keresteci after all.

Patient B's account of DeLuco's erect penis having a "kind of a crook" is but one line of evidence, says Humphrey. So vague, he says, as "not to bother calling" Keresteci.

Patient B is among four women who have levelled sexual complaints against DeLuco, 57, of Sault Ste. Marie.

She claims she and he were part of a *ménage à trois*, after duets at her home and his office. That's how she knows of that "kind of a crook."

Prosecutor Pat Band has suggested Keresteci found DeLuco's erect penis veers to the right with a "slight dorsal curvature."

"Your penis is not straight as an arrow and no one would characterize it as such," Band told the doctor on Monday.

"I would," DeLuco shot back. "Looking down on it, it deviates neither left nor right."

At issue are identity and, pardon me, hard evidence.

This case is mostly he-says-she-says, except for recordings of horny voicemails that Dr. DeLuco left for Patient B. So the cut of DeLuco's jib may resurface in final arguments today.

Meantime, we newshounds are left with nothing but to debate penile tendencies outside the College Street hearing room.

Just what constitutes a crook? Left, right? Up, down?

Should you worry if your erection goes south whilst the rest of you goes southeast? Remember Paula Jones? Her lawsuit claimed she noticed "distinguishing characteristics" when Bill Clinton offered her his lance of love in Little Rock.

Well, we know Clinton leaned to the left.

But what is a normal erect penis, anyway?

So when I get back from the hearing, I call Dr. Robert Stubbs at his Yorkville surgery. Few know penises like Dr. Stubbs. He has lengthened more than 550 of them.

"Very rarely do we see a perfectly straight penis," he tells me.

Usually, it has an upward tilt, especially when it is young. Often a fella's aim is high *and* wide.

Blame your *corpora cavernosum*.

Imagine your penis is buttressed by balloons on either side. If one balloon is blown up bigger than the other, what happens? Your penis bends the opposite way.

Mostly to the left, Stubbs has noticed. The right *corpus cavernosum*, a sort of tube, usually is bigger.

"It's like one of your feet is a bit bigger, one of your hands is a bit bigger, or one of your ears," says Stubbs, who once studied in China with a Dr. Long. "It's natural."

Maybe you "corkscrew." Double curve. Rare, thank God.

"Down is rare, too, where the head points toward your toes."

In an early Kinsey study, only 20 percent of men reported a straight penis. Many of them likely had a wee curve they never noticed.

Certainly, vaginas don't notice. Even sharper angles. Indeed, a short upturned penis really hits the G-spot.

Urologists say don't get bent out of shape, excuse me, unless sex is difficult or the angle is growing.

Sometimes, shudder, you wake up with it.

Say, if you slammed a door on your erection the night before and crunched your *corpora cavernosum*.

If it's real bad, it likely is Peyronie's Disease, named after a French doc who stumbled on it in 1743. Start worrying if you zig or zag more than 30 degrees. At 90 degrees, I think I would call 911.

Peyronie's plagues only 1 percent of men. One of the lucky few? An unkind cut likely awaits, though there are new traction devices. Otherwise, gents, that hitch in your post is perfectly normal.

It's us straight guys who are the freaks.

TECHNOPHOBIA

I Tweet Therefore I Am
(March 26, 2009)

Twitter: A succession of chirps as uttered by birds(ITL)
— Wiktionary

Demi Moore's ass introduced me to Twitter this week.
    Up to now, I've ignored the social networking fad in hopes it will go away, like pet rocks, boy bands, and beanie babies.

Sadly, there is no sign of this happening. Twitter nearly twoubled from six million users — a.k.a. tweeters or twitterers — in January to 10 million last month. One of them is Ashton Kutcher, the frisky young husband of ageless Demi Moore.

Like all tweeters, he spends way too much time answering Twitter's eternal question, "What are you doing?"

This week, for instance, he played peeping Tom with his wife.

Then, for all the world to see, he posted a pic of Demi's bikini-clad posterior on Twitter with the caption: "Shhh don't tell wifey."

The couple was in the Turks and Caicos Islands for the nuptials of her ex, Bruce Willis, 54, and lingerie model Emma Heming, 30.

Kutcher, 31, typed: "Watching my wife steam my suit while wearing a bikini. I love God! I'm not wearing the bikini, she is — that's what makes it so glorious."

Moore tweeted back: "He is such a sneak and while I was steaming his suit too!"

Ooooo! (Shiver!)

All sorts of questions come to mind. Such as: have you ever seen a nicer 46-year-old ass?

Also: Bruce's bride is 24 years younger than him?! Is it twu wuv? Or is he just a dirty old tweeter?

And: just what is Twitter, anyway?

Let's stick to the last one. AP says twitter.com is "a website offering a free real-time, short-messaging service. Users can post messages of up to 140 characters that are sent to interested recipients via computer or cellphone."

It's like a giant chat room. Instant texting — except everyone can tune in.

You "follow" the doings of friends, lovers, and celebrities. They, and others, can follow you. You tweet about any thought or action from the mundane — "I flushed" — to the meaningful — "OMG, I just drove off a bridge!"

Singer John Mayer twittered the other day that "I was sitting with my legs crossed for too long and my penis fell asleep."

Lovely, yes. And when it woke up, Jennifer Aniston was gone.

I'm not surprised Jen left him. He's a tweirdo. Reportedly, she was sick of all his twaddle.

It's everywhere, like the bubonic plague. Mayor David Miller is a twer.... I mean, twitterer.

As I write this, he has tweeted 11 times in an hour. He responds to a tweet from ex-Barenaked Lady/cyclist Steven Page.

"Yes!" exults Miller. "Dedicated bike path, pedestrian path, transit line, right across Queen's (sic) Quay. Better get back to my meeting...."

You do that, Mr. Mayor. Get back in there and screw us drivers some more. Quit wasting taxpayers' time twittering.

I bet Maxine X's tweets are more interesting. She's Canada's top fetish porn star. I've had the pleasure of hugging her a coupla times. Now she wants me to tweet her.

I take a peek. "Getting ready to shoot with a new bondage model today!" says Maxine, all a'twitter.

Sheesh. You don't suppose that's the "meeting" the mayor was tweeting about?

You never know. Welcome to Twitter. Welcome to the Twilight Zone.

People have proposed marriage there. They've delivered babies, blow-by-blow, play-by-play, tweet-by-tweet ("Gimme the damn drugs!!!!").

A California exec went on Twitter rather than call the cops when he heard a burglar. "I really am wondering why I haven't freaked the F out."

Because you're a meat-head.

A newly hired twitterer tweeted about how she liked the salary, but hated the job. Tragically, it was read by her new boss, also a twitterer. Moral: thwink before you tweet.

A bored juror posted pix of the murder weapon on Twitter. Shaquille O'Neal tweets at half-time. Barack Obama did it on the campaign trail. Britney Spears does it on tour.

Newsrooms are hardly immune. Our editorial page editor Rob Granatstein twitters.

The Rocky Mountain News covered a child's funeral via Twitter: "Earth being placed on coffin. People again are sobbing."

Boy, oh, boy. Now you can Twitter your life away from cradle to grave.

Pretty soon, you won't have to actually meet any people — ewwww! — at all.

DVD: Darn Vile Doodad
(January 7, 2003)

At Second City a few nights back, a song in one of the skits really hits home. Paul Constable and Pat Kelly sing, in part:

> *We're two guys without hope. Two guys without hope.*
> *These days we work more and more and seem to be making less.*
> *It seems technology is the cause of all our stress ...*

I guess!

Get my first DVD player for Christmas. A sleek, silver Sharp. Hook 'er up best I can. Nothing.

The manual starts promisingly: "1. Press the POWER button. The power will turn on."

Got it. But then it says things like: "If your TV does not have RCA type audio and video input jacks it is still possible to connect this DVD player to your TV's 75-ohm coaxial antenna terminal using a Stereo Audio/Video RF Modulator ..."

Pardon? I call the Sharp helpline.

"This book is Greek," I tell Laura Perez, 21.

She sounds puzzled. "I don't know how you got a Greek manual, sir. You sure it's not French? Mine's English."

No, no, I don't mean it's actually Gre ...

Laura has a lovely, dry laugh. She tries her best. But the DVD and my circa 1990 Zenith just won't talk.

"Maybe it's the TV," says Laura.

She puts me on to Sharp product manager Frank Koka, 40.

He listens to me vent a while about the manual.

"Well, I can see why most people, many people, would not understand that," he says gently, after I read him one dense paragraph.

"What the hell does o.h.m. stand for?" I demand.

"It's not o.h.m. It's a word. Ohm."

"Like ohm on the range? Ohm sweet ohm?"

"Yes. It's a measure of electrical resistance."

Oh my.

The trouble with electronics manuals, Koka tells me, is many are translated from Japanese, with tangled results. And some technical writers, he says, "overestimate the user's understanding, in terms of nomenclature or the product they're trying to describe."

I look up "nomenclature." It means a system of names.

It's on the same page as "non-functional," which, as Christmas fades, still describes my DVD.

And "nonentity," which is how I'm starting to feel in these technology-mad times.

Back in the newsroom, I corner Maryanna Lewyckyj, 42, our "Consumer Alert" columnist.

Tell me I'm not alone, Maryanna. Tell me the world has not finally gone to the geeks.

"Well, they are the modern-day hunters," she says, pity in her voice. "True, you can hunt these days to show your masculinity, but it doesn't impress many women. Now the alpha male is the guy who knows the most about electronics."

Maryanna fell for it, anyway. She lives with Larry Gillespie, 48, from our computer room. She says Larry even talks techno in his sleep.

Most of us cry out things like "Go for help, Lassie!" or "Not now, Raquel!"

Larry says, "We have to boot C system off B!"

So that makes Larry a mighty hunter? What are the rest of us? Spear carriers?

I know Larry and his computer colleagues smirk inside whenever I call about yet another laptop disaster.

I reach techno-guru Jim Carroll at a ski hill in Collingwood.

He writes and gives lectures about this stuff.

"You are not a freak," he tells me down the line. "There are so many people out there like you, it's stunning. We're the last generation (he's 43, I'm 47) in the history of mankind not to have grown up with computers. We've had a very unique relationship with technology. We've seen some ugly stuff. You're not an idiot."

Well, now I feel better. But I still can't use my DVD.

So I recruit a coupla friends. They are of a later generation, but they can't figure it out, either.

I call Darcel Tellis, 36, a Scarborough TV repair guy.

He is at my house three times, testing remotes. No luck.

They're coming to get my TV this week.

Darcel thinks he can make it talk to my DVD if he can get it into his shop.

Meantime, I'll read a book. Or whatever alpha males did before DVDs and such.

Maybe I'll grab a spear, go into the woods and try to bring down a moose.

Now Where Will Superman Change?
(March 2, 2007)

In storms like this, a phone booth is a beacon.

Fear not, frozen, weary traveller, it says. *Here is a light in the dark. Here is shelter from the wind. A shelf to rest your burden. A human voice to calm you, for just 25 cents. Folding doors to shut out the cold world. Something to read.*

In my Carleton University days, I knew a guy, a fellow student, who lived in and around a phone booth. Rent was zilch and he could call his mom whenever the urge struck, which, not surprisingly in his case, was quite often.

A phone booth saved Tippi Hedren from deranged seagulls in *The Birds.*

Maxwell Smart used a booth to enter CONTROL headquarters in TV's *Get Smart.*

It's how Harry Potter gets into the Ministry of Magic, how Bill and Ted took their Excellent Adventure.

In *2001: A Space Odyssey*, Heywood Floyd calls his daughter on Earth from an out-of-this-world video phone booth. It cost him $1.70.

Most famously of all, Superman uses one as a change room.

Even for us mortals, phone booths are part of our psychic landscape. So, where the hell did they all go?

On the way to work from Scarborough yesterday, I counted exactly two all the way down Kingston Road. They stood together, metallic twins, west of Guildwood Parkway.

I spotted a sprinkling of the open-air phones and perhaps I missed a booth or two. But no more do phone booths wait to embrace us on every block.

Britain keeps its classic red phone boxes mostly for tourists.

Canada's string of pay phones is shrinking by 4 percent a year. In 1998 there were 185,100. Now there are fewer than 130,000. A fraction of those are friendly booths.

The title character of the 2002 film *Phone Booth* was said to be Manhattan's last, though actually there's a handful left.

Later this year, Finland, home of Nokia, will become the first nation to ditch pay phones altogether. Why? Cellphones, what else? The same gizmo that makes people drive slow in the fast lane on the DVP.

At this time last year, 16.6 million Canadians had one.

"Pay phones are on the way out," says analyst Jennifer Simpson, 28, at Yankee Group in Boston. She's from Mississauga. "They'll be used on a minimal level, mostly for emergencies, if cell towers go out, for example. Or in places like northern Ontario, which don't have the coverage."

Or if you're a mobster and don't want to explain your cellphone bill to the coppers.

Or if you're a collector. Old booths are popping up on the web, some for thousands of dollars.

I have my eye on a 1950s model with bifold door, overhead light, ceiling fan and comfy seat, for just over a grand. It is like the one 25 South African kids used to set the first how-many-can-you-stuff-in-a-phone-booth record in 1959.

Ah, the good ol' days.

Even not so ol'. A lonely booth in the U.S. Mojave Desert earned cult status when its number was posted on the web in 1997. Folks lined up in the blazing sun to take calls from perfect strangers. Park rangers removed the booth.

Another one bites the dust.

Soon, they will all be gone. Only the cold, unfeeling open-air pay phone will remain, though I doubt for long.

My bet is on a new invention, the Cell Zone, a sound-proof booth where you can gab on your cellular even in a noisy bar.

Bell Canada, naturally, has a sunnier view of the pay phone's future.

Spokesman Paolo Pasquini, 34, concedes cells are king, but insists pay phones also have their place. They are now concentrated in demand areas. Malls. Varieties. Subway stations. Hospitals.

The demise of booths, he says, is just evolution. They are hard for wheelchairs and easy for vandals.

New pay phones are nearly smash-proof, can be used by the deaf, will tell you if there's an Amber Alert, and will report in if they're out of order or underused.

All of which is cold comfort in a storm. God be with you, if you are stranded on Kingston Road and your cell is dead.

They Belong in a Cell
(Septempber 16, 2006)

"What's bugging you?" I ask my friend Lenny.

He is part-Micmac, part-Irish newspaperman, which makes him an ideal barometer of the public mood.

"Drivers with cellphones," Lenny says, sparks in his eyes. "They're death on our streets."

Funny how they test you for a driver's licence. They test you again if you are nearly blind or very old. But they do not test to see if you can steer a car and chat on the phone at the same time.

Some of us are blessed with that ability. Some of us can even chew gum while we're at it. But many, maybe most, are not so lucky.

Sooner or later we will all pay for their frailty, because surely the province will outlaw the practice outright.

This summer, I was in Newfoundland, which imposed such a ban in 2003, the first and so far only one in Canada. Two years earlier, a poll of Newfies found 95 percent considered cellphones a serious road safety problem.

True, cell reception on The Rock is terrible. And most drivers are occupied watching out for moose. But still …

In a week of driving around the Avalon Peninsula, I saw not one ban buster. I saw none of the following creatures, common on the byways of Toronto. You know who you are.

The Invisible Menace. Look over at the slow Saab in the next lane and, holy Goteborg, there's no one in the driver's seat. The IM is so immersed in his call that he is slouched below the window line.

Look closer. The only sign of life is a hand rising from the shadows to the steering wheel and maybe the top of a cap.

The Wireless Lover. All the usual symptoms of amore, but in two tonnes of steel. Easy to tell. They blow kisses into the receiver and meander to the beat of "Unchained Melody" at 30 km/h in a 70 zone.

Or, when rescuers prise a WL's lifeless body from the telephone poll or the ditch, his face is fixed in a dreamy flush.

The Desperate Housewife. Not the kind on Wisteria Lane. This DH is in the van in the Loblaws parking lot, groceries and kids all over the back seats, hair in curlers, mascara smeared, sweatshirt all sloppy. Yackety-yacking on the phone. To the daycare? The dry cleaner? The dentist? A girlfriend? The mailman?

Who knows. Just stay put until she has careened from the parking lot. Then leave slowly, carefully, eyes wide, especially mornings in the 'burbs.

Parking lots are crawlin' with 'em.

The Lethally Lost. Warning sign: Car moves in fits and stops. LL is getting directions over the phone while peering up at street signs.

Read their lips. "Wha-? Wher-? Boulev-? Lef-? Ri-?"

The worst cases also consult a map in their lap. They are on the road to ruin.

The Phone Card. This joker is regaling someone with his wit. The quips are cracking him up. Gesticulations. Guffaws. Gyrations. The PC exhibits many symptoms, except sensible driving.

Look, no hands. The PC is laughing all the way to the bank. The snowbank.

The Phone-y Baloney. They just pretend to be on the cell. "Look at meee! I'm important. I have friends."

You can tell by their lips, which move out of sync with normal conversation, like Cary Grant talking to Rosalind Russell on the phone in His Girl Friday.

We all knew Cary wasn't really talking to Rosalind.

But imagine those two driving their Packards up the DVP, with cells in their ears.

Listen to me, you great big bubble-headed baboon! So, can we ground such highway hazards, drivers who cannot multi-task, who zone out when they dial up?

Fat chance.

So, MPP John O'Toole has another idea. The Tory transportation critic has tabled a private member's bill to ban hand-helds.

I reach him on his cell.

"In your car, Honourable Member?!"

"Never." He's at home in Bowmanville.

In his files are studies showing IMs and WLs and DHs and their ilk are four or five times more likely to crash.

"They've done tests and it's similar to being impaired."

New York State has a ban. So do more than 40 countries.

O'Toole would allow hands-free phones, though this will not save us from those who jump into a phone call like it is a hot bath. Remember the fuss about seatbelts? Well, O'Toole sees similar enforcement, with education and police blitzes.

One thing for sure. A ban would remove another peril from our streets.

People like me. The ones cursing, dodging and glaring at cellphone zombies when our eyes should be on the road.

(Note: Ontario banned handheld devices in cars in 2009)

I Got My Mojo Working
(September 21, 2007)

This week I am in Mojo training. It is not what you think. Not voodoo. Or techniques in bed.

Mojo, as in Mobile Journalist.

Not just writer or lensman. Both. Plus videographer, blogger, ambulance chaser, chat room chatter, TV talker, man-on-the-street prowler, and wireless geek. A sort of jack of all journalism. They tell me this is the future of newspapers.

Pen and pad? Pshaw! Soon my Ford will be a Mojo Mobile, cluttered with laptops, radios, Blackberry, several kinds of cameras and recorders, and assorted other techno crap. And makeup, to look pretty on screen. For me, a whole trunkful.

Many old-time journos bellyache about these new duties, but I can't wait. By the end of training, the number at the bottom of my column will be a hotline for myriad needs.

I will show up at your door not only to talk about your run-in with City Hall, or your 800-pound pumpkin, or your close shave with a flying saucer.

No, this is the Age of the Mojo. As of today, I am pleased to offer the following services:

Love Letter Writing. What I don't know about amore isn't worth knowing. I have joined dating clubs, sex addiction groups, adult toy workshops. I have covered fake orgasm contests and the Tie Domi/Belinda Stronach romance. Not necessarily in that order.

So, a Valentine's Day card to your wife will be a breeze.

> Isabel, ma belle
> You sure are swell
> Those lips so sweet
> I worship your feet

Fella, you'll be in like Flynn.

(Bonus coverage: Snappy greeting card messages, diary entries, resignation letters, notes to the teacher, and police confessions. With video, photographs, and links to *torontosun.com*.)

Neighbourhood Counselling. Gather the locals. I will come over and extol your area's virtues and explain how the media always overblows things. (Offer valid only in Scarborough.)

Fight City Hall. I have lots of experience with bureaucrats. We can talk about whom to pester and what exactly the hell is a junior assistant to the senior associate deputy district director.

Or, with my new Mojo techno talent, I can teach you how to retouch a photo so your local councillor is canoodling with a stripper. Guaranteed to get new sidewalks on your street.

Personal Trainer. I have played with a dwarf basketball team, ridden a saddle bronc (briefly), jumped out of a plane, bellydanced with identical twins, practiced with professional wife-carriers, arm wrestled the world champ, and judged cannonball diving.

You'll not find better credentials to whip you into shape. Okay, I have a bit of a tummy. We'll do a few situps and go for a beer.

Gossip mongering. A journo's stock-in-trade, though he never admits it. I can tell you juicy bits about all manner of politicians, sports stars, tycoons, movie stars, and, ahem, *Sun* personalities. For instance, Mark Bonokoski …

Well, you'll just have to call 1-800-MOJO and get in line.

Cure for Insomnia. Call me up and I will read you one of my political columns. Never fails. You will sleep especially well knowing I have interviewed you for six different kinds of media, photographed and Web-cammed you, mowed your lawn, taken out the garbage, patched your roof, cooked dinner, washed your car, read your kids a story, PVRed *American Idol*, written the report for tomorrow's meeting, and walked the dog …

What a brave new world.

So many ways to get your Mojo working.

Shunned by the Beautiful
(July 4, 2008)

BeautifulPeople.net has rejected me as a member.

I'm crushed.

"Dear MikeyMike," says the official snub. "The members of BP did not find your profile attractive enough this time around."

You're kidding! What's not to like about a "cuddly," 50ish, bald non-smoker who "enjoys long walks on the beach, romantic music, candlelight dinners, and the love of a beautiful woman."

What do they want, Brad Pitt?

"You are more than welcome to try again," says the veto, after three days of voting. "Perhaps with a better picture and more interesting profile text."

Screw you, buddy. And your 175,000 snooty members.

Right away I call my favourite shrink, Dr. Irvin Wolkoff, who is also cuddly and 50ish.

"Relax," he says. "You're not that ugly. I like the shaved-head look. And you wear nice trousers."

Thanks, Irv. But that's not much consolation, even from a noted psychiatrist. I mean, JoyfulPrincess didn't vote for me and her profile says, "I would not be where I am today if it wasn't for God."

What happened to "Thou shalt not shun plain people?"

So, how should I react to *BeautifulPeople*'s rebuke?

"You should feel chastened," says Doc Wolkoff.

"Because I'm homely?"

"No, because you applied in the first place. Never make that mistake again. They elevate pathological narcissism to a cultural art form. This is an odious, and horrible development in the world of online services, which I think are already a lot like picking chewing gum out of the old trough urinals at Maple Leaf Gardens. No matter how prettily it glitters in the trough, the flavour is gone."

(Irv got an A in Analogy at shrink school.)

"Besides, the guys (on *BeautifulPeople.net*) are probably all hung like hamsters."

There's a thought. Let's start our own club. *BountifulPeople.com*. We'd vote, too. Sort of a hung jury.

"But, otherwise, what do us homely people have to hang on to, Doc?"

"Ask any beauty expert. The core of beauty is personality. Be confident and present yourself to the world in a way that suggests not sick vanity, but that you calmly believe you are beautiful."

Will do.

First, if *BeautifulPeople* won't have me, maybe *uglypersons.com* will. My missus says it's a better bet.

I call the number. I'm suspicious. It's near San Francisco, in Marin County, which swarms with the likes of George Lucas, Van Morrison, Jennifer Aniston, Sean Penn, and Prince Andrew Romanov.

BP country. I've been there. They kicked me out.

A guy who answers the phone says he sold the domain long ago and he doubts it's still operating.

I try *uglypeople.com*, but it makes even me retch.

"Click Here to Find A Sex Partner in Your Area Tonight" does not help the beauty-is-only-skin-deep cause.

Same old, same old.

I'm sure there were "beautiful" cavemen and "ugly" cavemen, though nowadays "Neanderthal" is nearly always an insult.

The writer Petronius was arbiter elegantiae in the court of nutty Roman emperor Nero. Beauty was in the eye of Petronius.

This week, Fox TV and the New York Times got into the act. On its morning show, Fox used photos of Times staff that had been subtly "uglified." Normally, both men would be shoo-ins on *BeautifulPeople*.

But on Fox they got wonky noses, bags under their eyes, and yellow teeth. One acquired a receding hairline, the other bigger ears. This after a Times article took a shot at Fox's ratings.

"A hit piece," the Times culture editor said of the photos, but declined to go further.

"It is fighting with a pig. Everyone gets dirty and the pig likes it."

Ugly, ugly.

Actually, I thought the revised photos were an improvement. But I don't know much about beauty.

Except that, apparently, I'm not it.

WHAT'S NEW AT THE ZOO?

Waiter, There's a Rat in My Bowl!
(May 26, 2007)

Mario and Antonietta Rocco leave a hefty candle holder, decorated with angels, on their toilet lid downstairs.

This is to keep the rats from climbing out.

RATS IN THE TOILET!?

You might as well yell SHARK!

"I'm scared out of my mind," says the Roccos' daughter

Angie, 48, who lives with them. "You just don't want to believe it."

The bite marks are the worst. They scar the underside of the seat. Like a surfboard in *Jaws*. Something toothy. Something determined. Something big is trying to breach the Roccos' defences.

With some success. The bottom of the door from the bathroom/laundry also has been chewed up. Photographer Veronica Henri shivers at the sight.

Over there is the floor drain, where Mario, 84, saw the first rat a month ago. It had lifted the drain cover, sassy as can be.

Mario, who was on his way to shave, chased the bugger into the bathroom. But before Mario could lay hands on a suitable club, the rat threw him a sneer, leaped into the toilet bowl, and dived out of sight down the outlet.

Shudder. Two worries spring to mind:

(1) Rats can jump?! How high?

"Two to three feet straight up," Ed "The Exterminator" Bandurka tells me. "Depends how strong and old they are." A strapping Norway rat can execute quite a swan dive.

(2) You mean toilet-hopping rats aren't just an urban myth?

"It's rare, but it happens," says Ed, 37, a manager at Orkin/PCO. "Rats love to swim. In New York city, people actually install stoppers to keep them out."

Shudder. No more reading *War and Peace* in the can for me. This is like an eyeball in your stew. Or a snake in your sleeping bag. Or leeches in your pants. And I'm not even that squeamish. In the Amazon, I ate jungle rat for lunch.

We called it rat-atouille.

The Rocco women won't go to the basement without Mario, a retired and fearless mason. He has chased a second unwanted house guest, the size of his wrist, into that toilet.

Problem is, the rats are thinking penthouse. The Roccos have found food stashed behind the upstairs stove, including most of a loaf of Mario's home-baked bread.

"At first, we thought it must be squirrels," says Angie. "It had to be something big to carry that."

I hasten to add that the house, near St. Clair and Oakwood, is clean as a whistle. You could eat off the floors. Even if you are not a rat. But careful. The Roccos have put traps everywhere. Snap-traps. Glue traps. Poison. But the rats hoist the bait, including almonds, and skulk off unharmed.

"Rats are highly intelligent," Ed Bandurka tells me.

(So, that's who's been leafing through my *War and Peace*.)

One time, at a grocery, Ed's team had to deal with a pack of marauders who ate only red peppers. Not green ones. Not yellow ones.

"Wanna catch a rat?" Ed once told me. "You gotta think like a rat."

Speaking of which, what is City Hall doing about this?

Deserting a sinking ship?

"For God sakes, rats are coming out of the toilet," Angie wrote in desperation to local councillor, Cesar Palacio.

Last week, the city flushed the area sewer with water. Still, fresh teeth marks appear on the toilet seat. The Roccos smell a rat. As usual, this is a turf war. Rodents are the responsibility of four different city departments, depending where they come from.

Parks and Rec, for instance, if they besiege your house from a parkette. Sewer rats, which these most certainly are, usually belong to Public Works. Once they cross your threshold, though, they are private rats and your problem.

But what if they come to you direct from a city sewer along a porcelain highway? Palacio has convened a meeting of experts at the Rocco house next Wednesday to figure it out.

Last year he proposed rodent control come under one roof. Sort of a united rat patrol. City council voted it down. Figures. That way, they stay out of the rat race.

And leave us with the crumbs.

Sharks in the Great Lakes? How Eerie!
(June 2, 2007)

You yell barracuda, everybody says, "Huh? What?"
You yell shark, we've got a panic on our hands.
— Mayor Larry Vaughn in *Jaws*.

Sharks!! Peter Worthington wrote movingly in their defence this week.

They are hounded, hunted, hated and misunderstood. Ask the shark lobby. Ask any shark apologist.

When they bite us, it is because we stupidly look like a seal. Or we muck up the water. Or we entice them with dangling legs. Or we pique their curiosity. Or we invaded their home.

Blame the victim.

Well, someone has to speak for the victims, including those of us who suffer from selachophobia.

Peter was right. I have an irrational fear of sharks.

Irrational? What is irrational about dreading a monster that ambushes us from the deep and has nasty, nasty teeth? What is irrational about loathing those lifeless eyes.... Black eyes. Like a doll's eyes. When he comes at ya, doesn't seem to be living. Until he bites ya, and those black eyes roll over white and then ...

Cut it out, Quint. Get a bigger boat.

Justin Timberlake is selachophobic and will not venture into the surf. Not even to frolic with Scarlett Johansson?!

Terrible disease, selachophobia.

Christina Ricci lives in fear a shark will squeeze through the filter of her suburban swimming pool.

The only shark I've seen in the wild was a whitetip from the portal of a submarine off Barbados.

"Lemme out of here," I begged the pilot, my mind muddled by panic.

I had nightsweats for days after seeing *Open Water.*

I count the days (58) to Discovery Channel's Shark Week with a morbid thrill. This year's lineup includes: "Ocean of Fear: Worst Shark Attack Ever." Plus, "Top Five Eaten Alive." Then, some idiot will try to hypnotize a Great White.

I'm gonna pass out.

Nothing on freshwater sharks, I see, but still you will not catch me more than ankle deep at Woodbine Beach.

Rumours sometime surface about sharks in the Great Lakes. (You're a hammerhead, Mike!)

Impossible? Well, bull sharks have eaten bathers in Central America's Lake Nicaragua. They've been spotted above St. Louis in the Mississippi and far up Australian rivers.

They are the only sharks known to thrive in fresh water. They are the grumpiest and most fearless of sharks. More testosterone than an elephant.

I have the jawbone of an eight-foot bull shark. God help us if one of these buggers decides to swim up the St. Lawrence.

"Monster Shark Terrorizing Lake Superior," said a headline in *Weekly World News,* a supermarket tab. It claimed a freshwater Jaws had gobbled a deer off Whitefish Point, Michigan.

It also reported Hillary Clinton had an affair with an ET. Let's get real.

There are giants in the Great Lakes, already. Eight feet and longer. But you yell "Sturgeon!" and nobody even looks up.

Could a bull shark get through the Seaway?

"It wouldn't have any trouble," Royal Ontario Museum ichthyologist Dr. Rick Winterbottom tells me. "In Nicaragua, they go up the river from the ocean to the lake through four series of rapids."

A few years ago, a wildlife officer brought Winterbottom a shark's jaw found on a bank of the St. Lawrence near the Thousand Islands Bridge.

Sheesh. Sharks off Brockville!?

"I told him one possibility was a shark swam up there, died, and left its jaws," the ichthyologist, 62, says, dryly. "Or, some tourist caught a shark in Florida, brought the jaws home in the back seat and by the time he got to the bridge, it stank so bad, his wife made him throw it out."

The catch, says Winterbottom, is the bull shark likes warm water and never ventures this far north.

"Nothing is ever impossible, but some things are incredibly improbable."

Small comfort, Professor, for a guy with selachophobia, who thinks Jaws might be patrolling off Cherry Beach.

"Frankly, I'd be more worried about crocodiles."

Whaaat???!!!

A Case of Illegally Parked Trunks
(May 18, 2006)

We are in Courtroom H. *H*, as in Heffalump.

Forgive me, Winnie the Pooh. You want nothing to do with this circus.

We are here because the city is trying to make an example of two elephants, Caesar, 19, and Limba, 43. Owner Mike Hackenberger, 49, and his Bowmanville Zoo, are accused of displaying them in T.O. contrary to bylaws.

Many animals are barred from city streets. Mongooses, for instance. Ostriches, alligators, anteaters, sloths, armadillos, kangaroos ... flying foxes?! Fear not, it's a kind of bat. Skunks, wolves, pigs, sheep, cattle, weasels, jackasses, too, though have you been to City Hall lately?

And proboscidae. Elephants.

So, last October 29, bylaw officer Peter Freeman showed up outside a wine tasting at the National Trade Centre. The event was to raise money for the University Health Network, which everyone agrees does noble work.

Limba and Caesar were there as a neat gimmick and to give Hackenberger a chance to tell people about his favourite animal and its fight against extinction. Also noble work.

Then along comes the city.

Testimony yesterday does not reveal who made the complaint, but animal control officers could see Limba from their digs at the Horse Palace next door.

"I arrived to find a greyish elephant that was larger than myself," testifies the reedy Officer Freeman.

I should say. Limba is 8-foot-10 and 7,652 pounds.

Officer Freeman, 41, did not even see Caesar, 9-foot-2, 8,000 pounds, who was nearby shmoozing with his handlers and his fans.

Nor did he take note of the five 6-by-4 display boards about elephants, the pamphlets or the zoo experts talking to folks.

This is key to the case.

No, you cannot ride an elephant to work. Or give your kid one for Christmas.

But they are allowed in the city for educational events. You must also be a recognized zoo.

I do not know what Officer Freeman and his superiors were thinking, but they laid charges. Serious business: $5,000 fine or you're caged for six months.

So here we are, in a sweltering courtroom at Old City Hall, booked all day for this idiotic case. Your taxes at work.

Silver fox Clayton Ruby is the defence lawyer. I do not know his fee. But it ain't peanuts.

Soon, city prosecutor Geoff Uyeno looks like he has been run over by a herd of, well, you know.

The hapless Officer Freeman has no evidence to speak of, no real notes, though he assures us the elephants seemed quite safe. But, he continues, "I wasn't satisfied that what I was seeing qualified as an education program."

He remembers one sign, though he barely glanced at it. All five are on display in court.

Thus, he still does not know that "elephants are very vocal, producing a wide variety of squeals, screams and high-pitched trumpeting. [But] 75 percent of the vocal communication uses frequency too low for humans to hear."

So Caesar and Limba will be able to make rude comments about City Hall, without us knowing.

Sure sounds educational to me.

And to Toronto Zoo CEO Calvin White, who testifies Bowmanville is an "excellent" zoo with a "fabulous" outreach program. And to three other zookeepers and a Guelph prof, who testify such events help save animals. And to Justice of the Peace Kevin Madigan, a terrier on the bench, who says it best near the end: "This is ridiculous."

So, after 6 1/2 wasted hours, prosecutor Uyeno folds his tent, so to speak, and suggests acquittal.

The judge agrees and for a second, I think the whole courtroom will rise and trumpet: "Yes!"

Now, let's be fair to Officer Freeman.

Ruby compares him to Inspector Clouseau and Sergeant Schultz on Hogan's Heroes.

But somewhere up the food chain, a bell should have rung. I suspect the city just wanted to throw its weight around.

All our problems. The guns, the gangs, the street-racers, the jokers who park on Kingston Road at rush hour.

And we go after the gentlest giant in the animal kingdom.

I may not know much about elephants.

But I know a croc when I see one.

Be Still My Bleating Heart
(October. 2, 2004)

The Royal Winter Fair is messin' with the wrong farm animal.

You just do not snub the favourite of pharaohs. The oldest friend of man, besides dogs. The source of more food world-wide than the dullard cow. The nurse-maid to Zeus, the nourisher of Gandhi. The bearer of mohair and cashmere. The neatest, cleanest, smartest critter in the barnyard.

The noble goat.

That bleating you hear is from goat farmers across Ontario.

The Royal Winter Fair, to cut costs, has dropped its goat show. No more ribbons for best billy. Goats are gone from Royal posters and programs. Wanna see a goat at the fair this year? Try the petting zoo.

"It's the last straw," says Michael Domingues, marketing boss at Woolwich Dairy, of Orangeville, which makes goat cheese. "This is a shot at goat breeders, a sign of disrespect. We sympathize with the budget problems, but why drop an entire animal?" (Ontario has 46,000 goats).

The Royal, which runs November 5–14, usually gets 200 goat entries. But it gets 500 sheep. So the sheep won. Though they're too stupid to realize it.

Woolwich threatened to halt funding for the fair's Goat Education Centre, where you can sample cheese and such. But this week the firm reconsidered.

"Why make it worse?" says Domingues.

I do not think the Royal has thought this through.

Ask the Chicago Cubs. They banned a billy goat from Wrigley Field in 1945 and have not had a sniff at a World Series since.

Maybe the Royal has bought into all that crap about goats being sidekicks of Satan, or that they eat tin cans.

"It's not the cans they want," says Garry Claassen, who has 212 milk goats near Teeswater. "They're after the label."

What, to read? I know goats are smart, but ...

"No, they like the wood components in the paper and glue. Goats are actually very clean animals and picky eaters. They would never eat garbage. They're browsers."

Mischievous, persistent, curious browsers. Always chewing pantseats or butting butts in cartoons.

They're cute, too. Names like nanny, billy, and kid. Even the females have funny beards.

"'Cute' is a problem for us," says goat farmer Cindy Hubble. "Actually, goats are quite beautiful, but we're not a backyard pet industry. We're a viable agriculture industry still finding its feet. The Royal's decision doesn't help."

Hubble has had fair success. She took the Reserve Champion Market Kid ribbon home to Stirling a few years back.

"This is a huge loss," she says of the Royal. "There's no other show with that profile. We hope they reconsider next year."

The fair says it will try, but money is tight. Meanwhile, it is trying to, pardon me, mend fences.

Education manager Sue Sheridan says she'll "step it up a notch" with goats. For instance, they will alternate with cows in the milking pen.

"We want to show they're incredible creatures, not only cute, but valuable to our economy and the changing demographic in Toronto."

Goat milk, meat, and wool are familiar to many immigrants. Only in North America do cows rule.

"It's a masculine thing," says Cindy Hubble. "Cattle are big, strong, impressive."

Also higher in fat and cholesterol.

The Royal a no-goat zone?

The pharaoh Cephrenes must be spinning in his pyramid.

So too the 2,234 goats buried with him.

Our Goose is Cooked
(June 14, 2009)

We need a new national bird. Enough with the goofy Canada goose, already. It's an obnoxious, noisy, ill-tempered, and foul fowl.

A national bird can't be a pest. Not to mention a black, grey, and white mark on our rep since being exported to unsuspecting lands like England, Scandinavia, and New Zealand.

This week comes the latest embarrassment: "Canada geese are essentially flying cows," says a Smithsonian researcher looking into their role in the ditching of a US Airways flight on the Hudson River.

In other words, they eat, they fly, they crap.

So New York City will kill up to 2,000 geese within 8 kilometers of Kennedy and LaGuardia airports. The roundup and gassing is timed to molting season, when geese can eat and crap, but not fly.

Slaughter our goose? *Branta canadensis?* The one on the centennial silver dollar?

At least let's recall our ambassador.

But no one cries foul. No animal rights activists march

on the U.S. consulate. Two thousand cooked geese is tons less crap on our beaches, parks, golf courses, and lawns.

"Good riddance" is not something you want said of your national bird.

But, wait. The Canada goose is not our official bird. Indeed, we don't have one. What an opportunity! Kill two birds with one stone.

Shake off our shame — and rename the Canada goose the "flying cow" — and finally crown an official Canadian bird.

But which one? There are 428 to choose from.

I need not look far. Our newsroom is full of bird-watchers. An odd bunch.

Photo boss Jim Thomson says things like, "I'll show you my hairy woodpecker if you show me your great tits."

Sadly, the great tit is a European bird. The hairy woodpecker lives here, but is a risky choice for national bird. We'll be on Letterman.

Thomson likes the red-tailed hawk. It's fast and has a steam-whistle cry, much louder than that of the Americans' bald eagle. Like many Canadian humans, its sexual encounters last five to 10 seconds. And it went green before that was fashionable — saving energy by flapping its wings infrequently.

Other candidates?

Boobies are common in Ottawa but are mostly tropical, so they're out. Our capital city is also full of bushtit, if you add in a couple letters. But it's mostly southern.

We have species of creepers, nuthatches, and cuckoos, again mostly in Ottawa. But I fear they'd be confused with twitterers, texters, and stiff-necked bloggers.

The albatross is native to our coasts. But who wants to wear their national bird around their neck?

The pink flamingo might work, but Scarborough has already claimed it. The grey jay is the pick of film critic Bruce

Kirkland. He's the kingfisher of newsroom birders, having sighted 680 bird species in North America since the 1970s, including the rare Middendorf's grasshopper warbler. Yes, the Middendorf's grasshopper warbler.

The grey jay, *perisoreus canadensis*, is a fine choice. It was called the Canada jay until some dusty ornithologists decided that was too risque. Its range is nearly all-Canadian, though it avoids Toronto. Which is very Canadian.

Says Kirkland: "They're cool, they're friendly, but they'll also steal your food. So they're passive aggressive, which I think is part of the Canadian identity.

"They're also talkative and have something to say — they're smart."

Like us, eh?

They're also called whisky-jacks, another Canadian hook. But to me they're overgrown house sparrows dipped in ashes. They don't even have the blue jay's lovely tuft.

We need something sexier, more dramatic. Something a marketing department can work with.

The common loon would do, but a national bird should never be "common."

No, I like the Snowy Owl. Its habitat is almost entirely Canadian, even the Leslie Street Spit.

Its graceful, unruffled, and regal. It looks like Canada.

And it won't crap on your lawn.

FAMILY MATTERS

Mother and Child Reunion
(October 1, 2008)

Our photo guys always tell me one picture is worth more than any column. For once, they're right.

Take a look: Zsuzsanna Toth and Mark Sardar. Mother and son. Together again. After 25 lost years.

I reached Mark mid-reunion in Budapest, Hungary.

"She's been hugging me and kissing me since I got here,"

MICHAEL PEAKE/SUN MEDIA

Mark Sardar reconnects online with his long-lost mom in Hungary.

Mark says, his delight loud and clear over 7,000 kilometres.

In case you missed my earlier columns, Mark's father dragged him off to Bangladesh from Budapest when he was six and never spoke of Zsuzsanna again. The boy grew up and came to Canada, not knowing if his mom was alive, not even knowing her name.

Mark, 31, his wife, Kim, and their North York neighbours, the rock band Pandamonia, asked me for help two weeks ago. Hungarian media picked up the column. Zsuzsanna's nephew heard it on radio.

Quicker than you can say "sour cherry and cottage cheese strudel," Mark was on a plane to Budapest.

The reunion happened at the national radio offices. Zsuzsanna brought him an apple.

"Hi, mom," Mark said.

"Words can't describe," Mark tells me. You can imagine. Mark speaks no Hungarian, Zsuzsanna no English.

Hugs and tears are universal. It was a noisy, joyous mess. She ruffled his hair. "I think she understands my body language," Mark says happily.

Then they drove back to Zsuzsanna's apartment building in the 7th District of Budapest, where she lives with her husband, a locksmith. Mark was a boy there.

"Wait a minute," Mark murmured, and without guidance he climbed to the fourth floor ...

... straight to the doorway of his childhood.

Like he never left.

Zsuzsanna whipped up cabbage rolls with sour cream. Then, chocolates and beer.

Long-lost friends and family streamed in and out. Mark's uncle managed a little English, but mostly it was hugs and kisses.

"They sure hug and kiss a lot over here," Mark tells me over the phone. "I guess I can get used to it. When I get back to Canada, I'm taking Hungarian lessons. Next time, I want to be able to talk to my mom."

Exhausted, he curled up in her arms. She stroked his hair.

"I was out for 12 hours," says Mark. "I've never had a better sleep."

Well, they say you always sleep best at your mom's.

In the morning, coffee and croissants (Hungarians invented them, you know, not the French) at the round table Mark remembers.

The small flat hasn't changed much, though his toy piano is long gone. She brought out the few old photos Mark's dad didn't destroy or take to Bangladesh. "I kept these for when you came," she told Mark through an uncle.

They toured the old neighborhood; and he remembers riding his bike.

When I called, they were in Budapest's beautiful Castle District, with national radio (MR-1) reporter Eva Bansagi. Eva and colleague Tunde Varga were first to pick up the story in Hungary last week.

"I'm just loving this," Mark tells me, fresh from lunch

of pretzels at a cafe. "It's so much more than I'd hoped for.

"I wish you were here."

In a way, we all are, Mark. Enjoy. Give your mom a hug for us.

Is This Family About to Be Dethroned?
(November 2, 2001)

Ian Crapper, a bank guy I know, has a great sense of humour. Good thing, given his last name.

When you're called Crapper, you look for silver linings and Ian's family long ago found a beauty. They claim a direct line to Englishman Thomas Crapper, who, as every schoolboy knows, invented the flush toilet.

For a year, Ian Crapper, 36, has regaled me with the story of this link to glory. But a shadow of doubt has fallen on Ian and his proud family.

Last week, in the, uh, reading room at home, I flipped through *Extraordinary Origins of Everyday Things.* Charles Panati's book traces everything from toasters to Silly Putty. Under toilets, Panati credits early Minoan royalty, Englishman Sir John Harrington and others.

No Thomas Crapper.

In a footnote, Panati calls the Crapper connection "purely fictive." He brushes off a key 1969 book, *Flushed with Pride: The Story of Thomas Crapper*, as satire.

Oh oh, I think. *Flushed with Pride* is a Bible for Ian Crapper's family. They don't think it's satire. They think it's biography.

Perhaps they don't know the *Flushed* author also wrote *Bust Up: The Uplifting Tale of Otto Titzling*, supposedly about the inventor of the bra. Titzling, allegedly, was assisted by a Dane named Hans Delving. Hmmmm.

I confront friend Ian.

"That's crap," he exclaims. "We have proof."

So yesterday, he walks from Scotiabank, where he's a manager in e-commerce, to defend his family honour at a Spadina Avenue diner called — what else? — John's. It's just south of College. The meals are heaping and cheap. It's packed.

Crapper pulls out notes. He's prepped.

"But first, Ian, tell me about your life as a Crapper?"

He has a lusty laugh like Ed McMahon's. "You learn to be positive, to see the humour in it," he says.

Humour indeed. Consider these snippets: At Ian's mom's class reunion, they listed everyone's maiden and married names: Nancy Daly Crapper, hers read.

Ian's dad, Murray, and the four kids were an amateur singing group. They were billed as the Von Crappe Family.

At Vancouver airport, with Ian on standby, the intercom woman said: "Paging passenger Crapper," then broke down in titters on air.

Ian's wife is Kirsten. Clarke. "The deal was," Crapper laughs, "that she could keep her maiden name as long as our kids grew up as Crappers." They're expecting their first in February. They're building a second bathroom in their Riverdale semi.

In Grade 8, Ian won a speech contest with the Thomas Crapper story. "The principal told me I had a wonderful imagination. He didn't believe a word of it."

Which brings us back to the current Crapper flap.

Ian admits he learned five years ago that Thomas Crapper didn't actually invent the flush toilet, just improved it.

Ian's description goes right over my head, but he says it was called the "valveless water-waste preventer." Patent No. 812. It debuted in 1884 at a health show in London. It flushed a sponge and 10 apples with crowd-pleasing ease.

And, says Ian, one of Thomas Crapper's sons emigrated to Canada and developed Toronto's first waterworks.

(*Sun* columnist and history ace Mike Filey says that's news to him. But, lo and behold, he finds a James Crapper, plumber, in the city's 1883 directory.)

Ian rhymes off Thomas Crapper "facts": plumber at age 14, privy provider for Buckingham Palace.

Give us your best evidence, Ian.

He pulls out an old photo. Thomas Crapper. "Look at the forehead," he says. "Now look at mine."

Okay, Ian, case closed.

Maybe Thomas Crapper was a great inventor. Maybe he was just a good plumber. Maybe he didn't exist.

But when Ian Crapper and his family get together, they laugh about the doubting Thomases. They gaze at the portrait of their famous kin on the bathroom wall.

"It's funny," Ian says, "that we've been given this humorous name, so we've been able to make light of life. What a gift. So many people take life so heavily."

Yes, Ian, there is a Thomas Crapper.

He lives in the hearts of all who proudly bear his name.

Tough Choice for AK-47 Mom
(January 6, 2006)

One of many troubling things about the Yonge St. shootings: where are the moms?

Fifteen young men battle it out on Boxing Day in the heart of the city. Beautiful Jane Creba, 15, dies. Six wounded. Fifteen suspects, give or take. Fifteen families. Fifteen moms. Surely some of them know.

Not one has stepped forward.

Not one has taken her son by the ear and marched him down to a lawyer's office or a cop shop.

I wish they could spend a few minutes with the AK-Mom.

"They aren't doing their kids any favours by not turning them in," she says. "If you're raising a teenager, you can't be a wimp. You have to do what you know as an adult is right.

"What I did should be a clear statement to them. They should do the right thing."

What she did has the town talking: she squealed on her 17-year-old son.

Tuesday night she found an AK-47, clip at the ready, nestled on his bedroom pillow. She took the gun to 55 Division in a bag. They arrested the kid soon after.

"If he needs to go to jail, he goes to jail," she tells me in a lounge above the Hard Rock Cafe at Dundas Square.

Here, she's briefly joined an AM 640 panel called "Silence The Guns." They applauded her when she sat down.

From the window we can just see the mounds of plush toys and notes and flowers that rest where Jane Creba died.

"Even before the shooting," says the AK-Mom, "I would have done the same thing."

And he's not mad at her. He sends that message via a Salvation Army officer at youth court on Jarvis Street yesterday.

Courtroom 1 is too dark. The clerk has talked of adding lights to make it less sombre. Well, there's nothing cheery about kids gone wrong.

James Bubba sees his share. He is the justice of the peace presiding over the AK-Kid's bail hearing. But first a 15-year-old (alleged) mugger. Then two girls whose crime is unclear, but which has them a-twitter.

The law says we cannot identify them, or the AK-Kid, who arrives cuffed and corn-rowed six foot two of troubled road.

"I love you," murmurs the AK-Mom. She is slim and has red hair, round glasses, and hazel eyes.

The kid smiles and starts to reply, but an officer cuts him off. No talking in youth court. And stand up straight.

Then back to jail in Hamilton.

Next appearance in two weeks, on 13 weapons charges and cocaine possession.

"I just hope he gets the help he needs," the AK-Mom, 53, tells the press. Her son was diagnosed bipolar two years ago, she says. He is, as they say, known to police.

A lawyer hustles her away. She sneaks out the back.

The AK-Street is a quiet, quaint block near Jones and Gerrard. The AK-House is tiny. Home to the mom, her son on the ropes and her seven-year-old girl. Dad and Mom are still married, but he left to run a tourist shop in Jamaica.

Dreamcatchers hang in a front window of the little house. The kid makes them. He also plays piano, basketball, and slapdances, whatever that is. Or he did, says his mom, 'til he took up with rough company a couple of years back.

The street is not happy to hear of the AK-47 in their midst, but they applaud the mom.

"It should set a precedent," says Paula Aziz, 42, across the street, who has two daughters.

Paula says she'd have done the same thing, touch wood. "I'm bringing them up the best I can. Learn about your kids and what they do. Talk to them."

Says Aram Lee, 30: "She stepped up and more mothers need to do that."

Could you rat on your kid? Tough decision?

"It wasn't hard at all," says the AK-Mom when I catch up to her on Yonge. "I don't want a gun in my house, especially a big one."

She has a Cape Breton accent and she grew up with hunters. She is sure her son wanted her to find that gun. Earlier she had heard a "clicking" from the bedroom.

"It was a cry for me to save him from himself, before he did something with it."

Does that make you a hero, AK-Mom? No, she says. No more than a fireman is a hero for doing his job. Rescuing people. Putting out fires.

Just in on AM 640. Another shooting, this one on Birchmount Road.

Seems we're putting out fires every day in this town.

Moms Deserve a Hall of Fame
(May 11, 2008)

I was going to write about breasts today because I have to judge Miss Hooters Canada next week.

Then the lady with whom I sleep reminded me this is Mother's Day.

"Even more timely," I said, brightly. Mother's milk, etc.

"Then I will never speak to you ever again," she replied icily. "Or anything else, for that matter."

She is a mom and thus steeped in good sense.

Then I see loopy Lindsay Lohan's mom Dina is named a Top Mom on Long Island, New York.

Surely we can top that.

So, instead of breasts, I am writing about candidates for a Moms Hall of Fame, if there were such a thing.

Good or bad, they are stars in the maternal galaxy. Let's begin at the beginning with ...

Eve. Many of our moms have raised Cain, but none quite like Eve. Her adventures with Adam, Cain, Abel, and the serpent ripple in time, even to the opening credits of *Desperate Housewives*.

Madonna. A double entry. Both have experience with immaculate conception. One has sold 200 million albums, the other helped sell six billion Bibles.

Laura Secord. Mother of seven. If she had not left her kids with their wounded dad and hiked 30 kilometres during the War of 1812, we'd all have American accents.

Jocasta. Who? Mother of Oedipus, in Greek mythology, that's who. Fate led Oedipus to unknowingly slay his dad and marry his mom. This produced four kids with complexes. And bushels of money for Sigmund Freud.

Shania Twain. How a midriff can bounce back like that after pregnancy, well, it defies science. Twain uses Bag Balm, an ointment for cow's udders, to keep her skin soft.

Only a mom offers advice like that.

Edith Bunker. Sure, she always had to slink off to fetch Archie his beer, but Edith was a rock when the Bunkers faced moral crises.

Mother Nature. We make her life hell. Or we ignore her. We wilt her flowers, taint her food, invade her space, steal her gems. Yet, every morn we wake up and there she is smiling at us.

Marge Simpson. She's had brushes with kleptomania, cults, steroids, road rage, booze, gambling, amnesia. And she's always there for you when Dad is passed out drunk on the couch.

Britney Spears. Always there for you, passed out drunk on the couch.

June Cleaver. Now we're talkin'. Beav and Wally were lucky kids. No matter their mischief, she always had a nutritious meal waiting. Gosh, don't you wish moms still wore housefrocks and pearls?

Ma Barker. The anti-Cleaver. Mother to a gang of hoodlums, her own role is debatable.

One crook claimed Ma Barker "couldn't plan breakfast,"

let alone a crime. At any rate, she and son Fred were gunned down by the FBI in Florida in 1935.

Wilma Mankiller. A mom and the first chief of the Cherokee nation. But mostly she's on this list because of her cool name.

The Queen Mum. She put up with a lot in that pasty-faced family of hers. No wonder she drank. But she had scads of what we fancy in a mom: charm and wit and lovely hats.

Clair Huxtable. Lawyer, mother, mentor, and more than a match for husband Cliff on *The Cosby Show*. A prototype for the thoroughly modern urban mom, except with lots of free time.

Teri Hatcher. She skipped *30 Rock*'s "MILF Island" episode, but she's a hot mama on *Desperate Housewives* and in real life.

And, **Michelle Duggar**, 41, of Arkansas, who appeared in yesterday's *Sun*. She and husband Jim Bob await their 18th child.

They need to pick up the pace. The world record is 69 kids produced by **Mrs. Feodor "Stretch" Vassilyev**, a Russian peasant in the 1700s. These included four sets of quads.

So, there, the makings of a Moms Hall of Fame.

Other possibles include Maggie Trudeau, Jada Pinkett Smith, Jackie Onassis, Wilma Flintstone, Brangelina, Joan Crawford, Princess Di, Carmela Soprano, Mother Teresa, Mother Goose, Whistler's Mother, Mother Hubbard ...

Of course, you know exactly where your vote belongs.

Me, too.

Mrs. Strobel didn't raise no fool.

First Date? No Garlic
(May 7, 2005)

My son Jackson, 14, is about to embark on his first date. At least, his first date not involving bicycles, a set of swings or shared homework.

I have yet to meet the young lady, but "she is not too hard on the eyes, Dad."

By that, I gather Jackson is more worldly wise than I thought, though I have great respect for him. Especially since he hit six foot two in size 13 runners.

But these are dangerous times for a boy teen and his dad.

"Doing it at Age 14" screamed our headline this week over a StatsCan shocker. Survey said 12 percent of boys and 13 percent of girls had sexual intercourse by the age of 14 or 15.

Or claimed they had it. I bet the researchers got responses like, "Shure, man, I dunnit. Started when I wuz four."

Jackson's response was, "Whoa, they've got to be kidding."

The kid has his head screwed on right.

His first (official) date is to *A Lot Like Love*.

"I know it's a chick flick, Dad, but that's what she wants to see. Are all movie dates chick flicks?"

Well, no. My first, at 15, was a comedy western. James Garner and Lou Gossett Jr. in *The Skin Game*, 1971. Laughed so hard, I spilt Orange Crush all over my lady friend, a quiet blonde named Trudi. Never saw her again.

Lost in memory, I look up to see Linda Leatherdale at my door. Our business editor usually says things like "buy low, sell high," but she has another tip for Jackson.

"Beware of nudity."

Linda!

"No, really, it was a total shock to me. Just awful. And tell him to go easy on the cologne."

She explains. Her first date, an older feller, maybe 18, drove her to Toronto in one of those '60s landsharks. They had shrimp at Ed Mirvish's fancy lair, then saw *Hair*.

"It was Big Time for a little girl from Orillia," says Linda. Then Hair got to the full frontal bits. "Omigawd, it was the first time I'd ever seen a naked man."

No second go with that guy. Anyway, she hated his cologne.

Her next suitor suited better. No guff. He had her name tattooed on his ass. I will not tell that part to Jackson.

But I will tell him what Val Gibson says. Val, of course, is our columnist of luuuv.

She does not date so much as marry. Five men in all. She is Canada's most famous cougar, extolling the virtues of older women/younger men.

Nervously, I ask her about my son.

"He's a smart guy," she says. "He's going with what she wants to do. The snag with a movie is you can't talk. On the other hand, you have something to talk about afterwards, once you're done about family and hobbies and school."

"Activity-based" dating is usually best for teens, she says. Bowling, go-karting, anything to break the ice besides hanging out at the mall.

Val and other experts mostly agree on first-date musts.

Here's a dandy, Jack: listen to your dad.

"Teens shrug and we think they don't want to talk about it," says parent/teen coach Dr. Karyn Gordon. "But they do."

Boys especially may feel financial pressure. Two-dollar movies are long gone. And that's not all.

"Dating has always had pressures," says Dr. Karyn. "What's changed is it happens younger. Kids are expected to grow up faster and faster and they're just not ready for it emotionally."

Meanwhile, be clean and on time. Well dressed, whatever that means to kids these days. Listen as much as talk. Compliment her, but don't get gushy.

The night before, get a good sleep. Drink water. Take Vitamin A. No garlic. One website suggests reading a newspaper, so you have something current to say.

What about (blush) a first kiss?

"If she's okay with it, a light kiss goodnight is fine," says Val. "A thank-you kiss. He'll know during the evening how huggy she wants to be. Wait for that moment in the movie when it's a good time to put a hand on hers. Always test the other's reaction."

And whatever you do, Jackson, careful with the Orange Crush.

Oh, and Brush Your Teeth
(June 15, 2008)

My son, Jackson, just turned 18. And today seems a good time for a little last-minute advice from his old man.

Some of it I wish I'd imparted to the kid years ago, but was too busy, too tired, or whatever. Some he's sick of hearing. Some he might actually find helpful. Most he will ignore. You other dads are free to use it. Simply substitute your boy's name.

Here goes.

First, Jackson, always listen to your old man.

Stand straight and look everyone in the eye.

Be the best you can be. At least do the Canadian thing: go for silver and hope for bronze. You will always be gold to your dad.

Learn French. Just enough to say, "les Habs suck."

Pay close attention when encountering women: sometimes "yes" means "yes," sometimes "yes" means "maybe," sometimes it means "get over here, big fella," and occasionally "step any closer, and I call the cops." To be safe, assume "yes" means "no."

Avoid lawyers, politicians, and bureaucrats. Unless you become one. In which case, I disown you.

Vote your conscience. As long as it is not Liberal or NDP. Vote Green, if you must, until life beats the youthful idealism out of you.

Always serve at least two kinds of beer. Not everyone likes doppelbock.

Heed what Robert E. Lee said after Gettysburg. "It's all my fault." Even if it's not your fault, why waste energy blaming others?

This way, everyone sees you as a leader, even when you lose.

Rocky Balboa is a wise man. He said: "It ain't about how hard you hit, it's about how hard you can get hit and keep moving forward."

And don't say "ain't."

What goes around ...

Maybe some day you will be a dad, too. I never understood Marshall McLuhan, except for this: "Diaper backwards spells repaid. Think about it."

Yes, Jackson, think about it.

Let your word be your bond. But get it in writing from the other guy.

Wear a helmet. All the time. It's a deadly world. A Canada goose might fall on you.

Condoms are not party balloons. Always carry an extra. And a spare tank of barbecue propane.

Clean up your room. Aw, hell, forget it, I give up on that.

Big boys don't cry. Unless they're at a gas pump or

watching a Leafs game.

"Know everything you can about what you're doing," Fred Trump once said to his son. "Great and concise advice that I follow to this day," says The Donald.

Wear your hair however you want. Mohawk. Purple. Go nuts. Enjoy it while you got it.

Farting is a manly art, even a sort of code. I have done my very best to teach it to you. Use with caution around women and on job interviews, unless the guy interviewing you farts first.

Speaking of jobs, work hard. Better yet, make sure everyone thinks you're working hard, even if you are not. Do not worry that hard-working colleagues will steal your thunder. They are too busy, those losers.

As every Canadian dad says: keep your stick on ice. I'm too young to be a grandpa.

Avoid silly double entendres.

Do not pin all your hopes on the Leafs. Diversify. Watch the Jays now and then. Or the Raptors, Rock, TFC, or the Argos. In this town, you need a balanced sports portfolio. Stay away from Leafs futures and no-trade pension funds.

Avoid anything called Two-Dollar Tuesday.

Ethnic jokes are a no-no. They come back to haunt you. Look at Newfies. Now they're cracking wise about us.

If you must have black Goth fingernails, hide them when a *Sun* photographer shows up.

Be sick, not gay. (If you are of my vintage, dads, that means "be groovy, not sad.")

Do everything in moderation. Except the really fun things.

Oh, and did I mention? Always listen to your father.

But, mostly, listen to yourself.

Dad and the Man in Black
(May 10, 2006)

The Serenity Room is not where you want to be. A two-foot ceramic angel smiles down from a shelf on the wall. Lilac scents the air. The music is solemn.

There are many ghosts in here. The Serenity Room is where the residents of Maple Manor go when they are ready to die. This is where I find my father. The Man in Black, as usual, waits on a bedside table.

Maybe you have gone through this with your dad or mom, or soon will. We baby boomers are at that age.

"You see the shell of a man," says the soft, kind voice of a small-town nurse. "Sometimes you don't realize all there was inside."

So, let me slip Johnny Cash into the Serenity Room CD player and tell you a thing or two about my old man.

I hear the train a comin'
It's rolling round the bend
And I ain't seen the sunshine since I don't
know when

Little Joe Strobel was a shepherd, of all things, in pre-war Saskatchewan near Swift Current. In those dustbowl Depression days, he and my grandparents lived for a time in a grain bin. It was a Holiday Inn compared to the serfdoms of Hungary whence the Strobels came.

Much later, he traced us back half a millennium to when our duke packed up his serfs and moved out of Germany. The family tree took years to dig out of archives and church records. All dad ever found was serfs. Solid serfs.

Same out west, where he was born two months before the Crash of '29.

Wheat does no good in dust.

So they moved to the tobacco fields of Tillsonburg with all their Hungarian neighbours, with a stop on McCaul Street in Toronto where my grandmother made 25 cents an hour cleaning houses.

I've been everywhere, man
I've been everywhere

Mabee's Corners. McMaster, where he met my mom. Western U. Delhi, or Tobacco Town when tobacco was a health product. Pickering. Uxbridge. Scarborough. He was gym teacher and football coach at R.H. King Collegiate, now Academy, when the only uniforms were on the field.

A zillion Canadian kids moaned and groaned their way through his Health Hustle every day in class. Part of his job in phys. ed. at the Scarborough board was to dream up stuff like that.

Get a rock 'n' roll feelin' in your bones
Get taps on your toes and get gone
Get rhythm when you get the blues

Rhythm, Johnny? My old man could be a klutz.

Once, when we had horses, he face-planted in a wheelbarrow full of manure. Hands on the handles, mouth wide, managing an "Oh, sh ..." before he hit.

A lasting image of my teenhood is the old man making a beeline for the house, hollering for his toothbrush.

On a Sunday morning sidewalk,
I'm wishing, Lord, that I was stoned

The potheads are also in mourning this week.

My dad is, was, The Hero of Hemp. Every time I write anything about cannabis, people call to ask if I'm any relation. The *L.A. Times* put him on its front page. The CBC did a show, complete with "The Ballad of Joe Strobel." Kentucky even made him an honourary colonel.

This for a man who never smoked a doobie in his life, far as I know, but who saw a future for industrial hemp in the failing tobacco fields of Tillsonburg. So, in 1994, he got a licence to grow 10 acres of it on the family farm. He saw its worth in everything from clothes to floor joints, pardon the expression.

The narcotic in dad's hemp was so low your lungs imploded long before your mind expanded.

This did not stop true believers from raiding the candy patch. One left a bottle of wine in the mailbox in thanks.

Dad had to pay the Mounties to watch over harvest and he told nosy reporters the bales were in a "secret location." In fact they were in a neighbour's garage. The mystery just added to the legend. Now there is even hemp beer.

Tokers tagged along on his coattails, which made my dad a tad uneasy.

"Goofy," is what he called the stronger stuff.

Then the first stroke struck and the long decline began.

Every one I know
Goes away in the end

Funny, how we leave things. You are one in a million if you can squeeze in all the couldas and shouldas before a parent dies.

When they go, when night falls on Tillsonburg and the doctor is done, there is nothing for it but to wander down to the Royal Tavern and buy a round. To Joe Strobel, dead at 76.

Hey, karaoke man.

A little Johnny Cash, if you please.

HERO WORSHIP

The Movie Star and the Street Guy
(September 13, 2007)

The beggars of posh Yorkville have eyes as big as pans these days. All those film stars. All that spare change.

But a street regular known as Stress has struck gold. Pure Irish gold ...

— — —

Lunchtime. Eighty fans with Kodaks and pens are poised outside the InterContinental Hotel on Bloor Street.

The brass door spits out an A-lister. Colin Farrell. Not sure which dark, musky hunk is Farrell? Ask your wife. Her knees will buckle.

Anyway, Farrell is no snob. Patiently, he signs for everyone, then turns toward his chauffeured, charcoal Audi.

And there stands Stress. For years, he has haunted Yorkville and environs, peddling Outreach papers or mooching loonies.

"Peaceful, harmless guy," coffee salesman Bill Ikos, 32, tells me. Bill's hobby is photographing stars, often in Yorkville, which is how he knows Stress.

Bill is outside the InterContinental for the hunk/homeless hug.

"Hiya," says Stress. The film star's eyes light up.

Four years ago, he was in town shooting *A Home at the End of the World*. A radio babe offered $2,000 to anyone who could bring Colin Farrell (sigh!) down to the station.

Farrell grabbed the first rubby he saw and, bingo, Stress was $2,000 richer.

"Jump in," Farrell says at the reunion Tuesday.

I wish I'd been a fly in that Audi. Down to Front Street they cruise, to Europe Bound Travel Outfitters.

"Get him anything he wants," says Farrell, in that commanding Irish tone. He wears jeans and a black muscle shirt. Women staffers swoon. And not just over the bill, which comes to $2,100.

"Cool guy," manager Dave Mott, 36, tells me. "He doesn't act like a movie star."

Mott plans to tour Ireland by bike. "Don't miss the Ring of Kerry," says Farrell, 31, born in Castleknock, Dublin, a preemie at one pound, six ounces. Maybe that explains all this.

They roam the store, Colin and Stress, cracking jokes, trying things on.

"Like they were best buddies," says Mott. "The homeless guy was going around, grabbing stuff." Stress talks fast, hence the nickname.

"Whatever he needs," Farrell says again.

They pick out a $500 Arc'teryx coat, a North Face down sleeping bag, and a rolling backpack stuffed with socks, boots, and underwear.

"Everything top of the line," says Mott.

Yes, Stress will be the best-dressed beggar in Yorkville this winter.

But hold on to your baseball cap. There's more Stress relief.

"Where's the nearest bank machine," Farrell asks Mott.

He returns with a wad of $20s. And, he arranges to pay a year's rent on a nice room for Stress back up Bloor Street. The total tab must be near 10 grand.

Two and a half hours after Stress was swept off the street, he is back at Bellair and Cumberland.

"Where the hell you been?" says Bill Ikos.

"I'm all set up," says Stress, a tad frazzled. "This is my chance to get off the street." And he walks away.

"Amazing," Bill tells me. "You hear about someone like Al Pacino giving $100 bills. But to take a guy shopping and try to help turn his life around?"

Good thing Stress didn't run into Whoopi Goldberg or another star on the Yorkville panhandlers' "avoid" list.

"She never gives anything," says Joe Beard, who works Cumberland Street. I've known Joe for years. Gentle as a dove. Kiefer Sutherland usually drops him a $10 or $20.

The film festival is high season for these guys.

The Colin Farrell gesture has them abuzz, which is how I hear. No one in the actor's camp, I hasten to add, has tried to use it.

Funny thing. As Stress, Farrell, and a couple of aides leave Europe Bound, the security beep goes off.

Someone forgot to remove a tag.

Or it is the fates signalling thanks to a class act.

A Friend Indeed
(March 10, 2004)

You're at work. Look at the colleague to your right. You've toiled with him for years. You've had beers with him. You've bitched about the boss with him. You've met his kids.

Would you give up your kidney for him?

While you're mulling that, join me in the diningroom of a trim side-split on the south side of Acton. Try not to notice the backyard overlooks the town cemetery.

Dan MacCallum's face is shades of grey. He is 39. He has polycystic kidney disease.

Three weeks ago today, they removed one bloated kidney. Tomorrow, he finds out when his other one comes out. It, too, is useless. He goes to hospital for dialysis three days a week. He was a guard at the Metro West Detention Centre, before his health started going south.

Two years ago, 150 friends and family held a benefit barbecue. By then it was clear he would need a new kidney.

"Hey, Dan, take mine," everyone said as the beer flowed and old Metro West mates gathered behind the barbecue tent.

"All of a sudden I had nine kidneys waiting in line," Dan grins at me through the grey. "But I also knew they'd each had nine drinks."

Except Karen Middlebrook. She worked with Dan for seven years at Metro West. Went through two riots with him, countless Code Ones, and alarms.

"I'm A-positive, too," she told Dan. "If push comes to shove, give me a call."

"Be careful what you say," Dan smiled back.

He figured a donor would come from family. But his brother was found to have the disease. His mom was rejected. So was his wife, also a Karen, because son Eric, 8, has the disease, too, and might eventually need her kidney. A mom is always the best donor. (Dan's dad had a transplant in 1969. That kidney lasted 32 years.)

Last Boxing Day, Dan's kidneys quit. Dialysis saved him.

Word got back to the prison. Karen Middlebrook got on the phone. Dan and wee Eric were watching the Habs on TV.

"Know anyone who needs a kidney?" Middlebrook said down the line.

And Dan MacCallum sank to his knees. It takes five to seven years to get a new kidney in Ontario. There are 1,300 folks on the waiting list.

"She's an absolute hero," says Dan, his wife and two boys at his side. "We won the lottery with Karen. Nothing can repay the gift she's giving us. To think a (former) colleague at the jail rose to the occasion at the lowest point in my life."

The boys tuck into their grandma's chocolate chip muffins. Dan's just in from the doctor. Karen Middlebrook, 37, has dropped by before her shift at Metro West.

A handful of tests found compatibility. There's a double-check in three weeks. They need to be sure Karen's other kidney is strong. Then a hospital panel, including a shrink and a social worker, will test her motivation.

She has already met her transplant team coordinator. If all goes well, surgery will be this summer. Recovery is usually six to eight weeks.

You cannot look at Karen Middlebrook without wondering if you could make the decision she has made.

"You can't answer that hypothetically," she says. "Not until you're faced with it. People tell me they wouldn't be brave enough to do this, but how can you say that? What if tomorrow it was your child or your neighbour or your best friend?"

Jail guards, of course, form bonds like cops do. We send them our dregs. The child molesters, the gun-toting thugs, the killers, the rapists. You need to know the guard you work beside will be there when trouble comes, as it always does.

So, I guess that is part of Karen Middlebrook's thinking, though Dan no longer works at Metro West.

But there's more.

Five years ago, Karen had twins, 10 weeks early. One died. The other, BJ, pulled through but has cerebral palsy.

"A lot of people who didn't know me and didn't know my son gave their blood and their time and skill. That made this decision easy. It's as much the decision of a mother as the decision of a friend."

She watches Eric and Alec, 4, wolf down those muffins.

"I'd rather nurse an incision scar," she says, "than go to Dan's funeral."

(Note: The transplant was a complete success)

Quest for Father and Son Warriors
(November 26, 2001)

Just when you think the world's gone cold ...

Gord Palumbo is in the basement of his highrise at 88 Erskine Avenue in North Toronto. Dim light and shadows cross rows of rough pine lockers. In a murky corner, in a pile of refuse, Palumbo spots a black plastic bag, little boxes spilling out of it.

"I knew exactly what they were right away," says Palumbo, 33. "My grandfather was in World War II and he had medals in boxes just like that."

Palumbo takes his find upstairs, gets some jeweller's polish, and wipes off years of grime.

Here's what he found:

- Two First World War service medals awarded to Private W. H. Cameron.
- Two Second World War medals. One is the Memorial Cross, for RCAF Pilot Officer R.H. Cameron, killed in action April 23, 1944.
- A yellowed pamphlet on the etiquette of wearing medals.
- Two lady's garnet rings. A handful of coins from Britain, India, Ghana, and Cuba.
- A mystery. And a quest.

"You have to do what's right," Palumbo tells me later. "It's important to find out who these belong to, to give them to the family. I mean, it's the least I can do for a man who died for my country."

I haven't heard anyone talk like that since Andy of Mayberry. I look for any sign of pretense. Nothing.

Maybe gallantry is not dead, after all.

For four days, Palumbo searches. Building managers can't help. Records have been lost.

The bag could have sat in that dark corner for 20 years. It's from Castle Jewellers, 2482 Yonge Street. There is now a card shop there.

The one Cameron in Palumbo's 28-storey building knows nothing of the medals.

Palumbo calls two Royal Canadian Legion halls and National Defence. No luck, though the military says it'll hold the medals in case any Camerons come looking.

Palumbo starts on the phone book, then gives up. There are 594 Camerons in Toronto alone, never mind the GTA.

Finally, he phones me.

I meet him on Erskine Avenue. He looks like a guy from Timmins, which he is. Polite, honest face. Construction boots. About five foot six. He's held a number of jobs but is back in school for geology.

Reluctantly, he lends me the medals.

Late Friday and over the weekend, here's what I find on his Pilot Officer R.H. Cameron.

From Johanne Neville at the Commonwealth War Graves Commission, I learn he was a gunner. Pilot Officer didn't necessarily mean pilot. He was in a four-engine Stirling bomber that went down on a mine-laying mission in Denmark. It was a Sunday.

He was 20, from Toronto. He was RCAF, attached to the 149th Squadron of the Royal Air Force. Six others died in the Stirling, five Brits and an Australian, says Stephen Hayter at the Air Training Plan Museum in Brandon, Manitoba. The men lie in a common grave at Svendborg General Cemetery on the isle of Fyn in southern Denmark. It is 30 kilometres from the German border.

R.H. stood for Roderick Hugh. No record of next-of-kin. Seven weeks before D-Day, a lot of airmen were dying and verification records were sketchy. But it's likely the Memorial Cross went to his mom. It was custom for the mother and/or widow to get the silver medal, with its purple ribbon, says Major Jeff Forgrave in National Defence's honours and awards section.

Presumably, Roderick Hugh Cameron's dad was the W.H. of the First World War medals.

How the father's and son's medals came to sit in litter near Gord Palumbo's locker is anyone's guess. But privacy laws and bureaucracy make tracking surviving relatives tough.

Someone at Veterans Affairs tells me they might find Roderick Hugh Cameron's file by Christmas — but can't give out any names of kin anyway.

"Your best bet," says Forgrave, "is to publish what you know and see what happens."

So that's what I'm doing.

The experts aren't hopeful. Maybe the family line ran out.

But let me know if you can help get these medals where they belong.

A young man with a warm heart has them all polished up.

Medal Mystery Ends Happily
(December 14, 2001)

Our mystery medals are in their rightful home. They're with a kindly little grandmother near Barrie.

I wrote on November 26 about Gord Palumbo, who found a bag of war medals among debris in the basement of his highrise.

There were First World War medals in the name of Private W.H. Cameron and Second World War medals of Pilot Officer R.H. Cameron. The latter was killed in 1944.

Palumbo, 33, enlisted my help to find the Camerons' kin. The column prompted a rush of tips. We chased leads all over, including one in Kirkland Lake that looked surefire. But nothing clicked.

Then, Thelma Parsons called me from veterans affairs in P.E.I. and restored my faith in public servants.

"I've got it!" she yelped into the phone.

Deep in the VA files, she found an E. Dore listed as W.H. Cameron's next-of-kin. Parsons, 45, called across Canada for the right E. Dore.

Which brings Gord Palumbo and me to the living room of Elizabeth Cameron Dore yesterday. She lives in Sandy Cove, near the southwest shore of Lake Simcoe.

"Please, call me Betty," she says. She is 80, 4-foot-9, with lovely, soft white hair. If you were shopping for a grandmother, you would look no further. She is the only daughter of William H. (Bill) Cameron.

Her brother was Roderick Hugh Cameron, a gunner on a Stirling bomber shot down over Denmark.

Palumbo gives her the medals and a few jewels found with them. He has polished them all.

For a minute, none of us speaks. The house is full of family photos. It looks fresh-scrubbed. It smells of Christmas.

"Oh, I can't believe it," Betty Dore says. She slides an amethyst ring on a finger.

"Perfect fit," I say.

"It was my mother's," she murmurs. "I've worn it so many times." Not since 1985, though. Burglars hit her home on Blythwood Crescent in North Toronto.

Palumbo's highrise is three blocks away. Maybe the thieves ditched some of their haul.

Betty caresses the First World War medals.

"My father used to polish these all the time," she says. "That's Rod's." She gazes at the Memorial Cross, given to her mother, Mildred, after her brother's death. She studies the long purple ribbon.

Palumbo clears his throat and blinks.

"I'm thankful, Gord," Betty says softly and goes to fix tea.

When I met Palumbo he said he wanted most to see a photo of R.H. Cameron, who "died for my country." So Betty gets out the pictures. In each one, Rod beams like the star of a Disney movie.

He was 20 when he died. And gangly — 124 lbs

on a five-foot-ten frame. Betty has been to his grave at Svendborg, Denmark. There is a semi-circle of markers for Rod and his crewmates.

In Sandy Cove, she stares out at the mist.

"He was kind, very gentle. He liked to ski. He liked to camp. He had a lot of friends. He had a girlfriend, too, Jane Barton. They were practically engaged when he left. We all went down to Union Station to see him off."

They never saw him again.

In letters, he chided her playfully for joining the Canadian Women's Army Corps. Not for a proper lady, he told her. She worked at army offices in the post office, where the Air Canada Centre now stands. She kept books in the boots section.

She was there when she learned of Rod's death.

"One of the officers came and told me. He took me up to the cafeteria and I cried and we had a cup of tea." Then she went home to Fairlawn Avenue, in Lawrence Park. She named her first son Roderick. He lives in Kitchener.

The photos of Betty's father come out. Bill Cameron cut an unsmiling figure. He was all army.

"I remember him talking about how horrible it was in the trenches," Betty says.

The main painting in the Fairlawn house was an oil of an artilleryman comforting his dying horse.

Bill Cameron was wounded at Ypres. He had a maple leaf tattooed on his right arm, then he went back to the trenches. In his 40s, he signed up for the Second World War He did office duty. He died in 1981. He was 84. Mildred died the next year.

Betty's husband, Charles Dore, died in 1971. She has three kids, six grandkids.

Three hip operations have slowed her down, but her mind and her wit are still razor sharp.

As we leave, she teases Palumbo about how quiet he's been.

She has a jingle-bell laugh.

Christmas, I think, has come early.

Brendon Knew the Score
(May 31, 2002)

Brendon deSouza knows exactly the battle he's in. A while back, he sat on his bed and wrote out his will.

He's 11.

In a voice quiet and wise beyond those years, he tells me what it said. We're sitting with his mom, Judy, 38, in the family room of their Mississauga home.

"I left my teddy bears to my sisters," Brendon says. "I left all my hockey stuff to my mom and dad."

Signs of the Maple Leafs are everywhere. A jersey autographed by them all. A plastic Cujo on a shelf. Brendon wears a Leafs shirt, atop sweat pants and bare feet.

A bandage peeks over the neckline. His cancer came back in January. The tube through which he took his drugs was removed Wednesday. Tomorrow, Brendon will join Lloyd Robertson to launch Sick Kids' annual 24-hour telethon. It airs on CFTO.

If Brendon has his way, he will wear a Leafs shirt. His mom leans toward a suit. "Maybe I can wear the jersey over the suit?" He looks hopefully at his mom.

Tune in, to see who won. My money's on Brendon.

He has leukemia, complicated by a quirk of chromosomes that hinders treatment. He has had chemo, radiation, and a bone marrow transplant. He's now on a drug, virtually experimental, called Gleevac.

Veronica Henri/SUN MEDIA.

Brendon deSouza, with mom Judy.

The prognosis, frankly, is not good.

But, "he's handling his journey with grace and determination," says Dr. Norma D'Agostino, 33, in Sick Kids' psychology department. She met Brendon at the hospital's Camp Oochigeas in Muskoka two summers ago.

Brendon has since become a sort of prince of Sick Kids. On his weekly visit for tests, he tours the place, dispensing hugs and cracking jokes.

"Which side of an elephant has the most skin?" he asks me. Pause. "The outside," Brendon chuckles.

"He has this great enthusiasm for life," says D'Agostino. "He's decided he'll enjoy every day until he can't anymore. He's an amazing kid."

Yes, he is. I wish you could spend five minutes with him. It would cure whatever ails your soul.

He sits still and straight in an armchair, and speaks with startling maturity about things no 11-year-old should know.

He tells me how someone took him to a room at Credit Valley Hospital October 7, 1999, the day he was diagnosed.

He found his mom and dad crying. "At the time, I didn't know what it meant, what I would have to go through."

A lot, it turned out, for a kid who loves road hockey and Cujo and is rooting for England in the World Cup. A kid who bakes. His banana bread is reputed to be astonishing. Sadly, his latest batch — 10 loaves — is gone before photographer Veronica Henri and I visit.

Now, he grins and tells me he has to make a list of people who want Robertson's autograph. His grandma is a big fan.

Hey, Lloyd, I'm thinking, keep your wits this weekend. Your co-host is no pushover.

"Brendon has a strong personality," says his mom. "I think he has matured much more because he's gone through this. He has a deeper insight into life than most kids his age."

And he has not lost hope.

"I want to be a goalie when I grow up," he says in a serious tone. "Or a banker."

Later: "I'll get past this one day. I just need to keep going."

He has great help, he says. His mom, his dad, Len, 42, twin sisters Jessica and Samantha, 9, his friends, his school, Sick Kids.

"Ever get discouraged, Judy?"

"I try not to, as much as I know the truth of the matter. I need to keep positive, but every once in a while, it hits me."

"Brendon?"

"No," he says quickly and quietly.

"Never? No 'why me?' No 'what's gonna happen?'"

"I think about it sometimes, but discouraged? No. Though it does get tiring with the TV crew shooting for the telethon and with radio shows and newspapermen ...

"Nothing personal," he adds, a twinkle in his eyes. They are rimmed by shadows. "Sometimes I wish I was just a normal 11-year-old boy, without all the attention."

He thinks a minute.

"But I think I was specially picked to go through this. To show people how to appreciate life. Lots of people say, 'what's the point of living if you're just going to die anyway?'

"Well the point of living is to enjoy life as much as you can."

He pauses again, looks me straight in the eye.

"I know how to live," he says.

Sure do, Brendon. Have fun on TV this weekend.

(Note: Brendon died four months later.)

Keep the Flame Burning, Billy
(September 11, 2002)

"Good Morning. It's September 11, 2001. Have A Nice Day."

It's the small things he remembers. Like that desk calendar in the dust and debris.

Billy Carlson smokes a Marlboro and looks out the fire hall door at 8th Avenue screeching by.

A year ago today, this hall, the Pride of Midtown, home to Engine 54 and Ladder 4, lost 15 men in the tower collapse. Everyone from this hall who went down there died. Now, their photos hang on the wall.

A year ago, Billy Carlson worked out of Brooklyn. His station lost five guys. He transferred here in December.

A horn blows and Engine 54 roars out into the dusk. Ten minutes later, it's back. False alarm.

Engine 54 still bears the scars of 9/11. New paint can't hide all the scratches, bumps and burns. They found Ladder

4 buried four storeys deep in The Pile. Its men had been trying to open the door of an elevator full of civilians.

Carlson, 36, lights another Marlboro. A year ago today, he started smoking again.

He was home in Brooklyn when the first plane hit, suiting up at his station when the second hit. Walking in full gear across the Brooklyn Bridge as shocked, ash-covered civilians fled Manhattan. And at Ground Zero 20 minutes after Tower 1 fell.

He bought a pack of smokes and started digging. Two weeks later he dug up a floor sign.

"It said 96 and that was a blow. I threw the sign. I thought, 'we're only down to the 96th floor after all this digging and not finding anybody.'"

At least not alive. Billy would carry a dozen or more firefighters from The Pile before it was done.

Billy Carlson is a fourth-generation firefighter. A year ago today, he lost 100 guys he knew.

Each day, driving to his new station, he passes Ground Zero.

In May, he happened to be in one of the surviving buildings around The Pile, which by then had become known as The Pit.

There was a marble bench. Once, he had taken a break from digging to sit there, deep in thought, knee-deep in dust. This time the atrium was spotless. You could see yourself in the marble.

"It was almost like it never happened, like the whole thing had been covered up. I know we're supposed to move on and everything, but I hope that doesn't mean we forget."

For an hour we talk. He stares out at 8th Avenue the whole time. Sometimes, his eyes are damp, his voice choked. His truck, Ladder 4, is shiny new behind us. Its predecessor's big, battered sign hangs on a wall.

"Never missed a performance" is painted above the windshield of Engine 54. It's the fire hall motto. The lights of Broadway are a block away.

Tourists drop by all the time. Everyone loves a firefighter. A young woman comes in, with a bandaged toe. Not a grievous wound.

She bats an eye at Billy Carlson, points to the toe. "You got anything for this?"

Billy gets a power saw — they use it to cut through roofs — and fires it up, a loopy grin on his face. The girl jumps, then grins back and turns to another firefighter.

Tired of all the attention, Billy? Tourists. Media.

"Sure. But by talking to you it lets everyone know the FDNY is going to keep responding, that there is nothing that could ever destroy our spirit."

In the kitchen out back, Billy Carlson's famous sauerkraut pork chops are simmering. This morning, a year from the day 343 firefighters died, he will be on duty with Ladder 4.

He knows the world will move on. It always does. After Pearl Harbour. After countless wars and tragedies.

"I just hope the spirit of the men who died will be remembered. That we hang on to the compassion that was demonstrated after 9/11. That the civilians, too, died for a cause."

At 8:46 this morning, maybe as you read this, bells across New York City will toll and everyone will pause. It will be a year after the first plane struck. Billy Carlson, if he is not on a call, will look at the faces on the fire house wall.

Chris Santora, 23; Sam Oitice, 45; Len Ragaglia, 36; Paul Gill, 34; Carl Asaro, 39; Capt. Dave Wooley, 54; John Tipping, 33; Mike Haub, 34; Joe Angelini, 38; Mike Brennan, 27; Jose Guadalupe, 37; Lieutenant Dan O'Callaghan, 42; Battalion Chief Ed Geraghty, 45, smiling as always.

When the bells stop, Billy Carlson will wander out to 8th Avenue and watch the world move on.

Keep the faith, Billy. Keep the flame burning.

The Last of the Fifty
(November 7, 2007)

Yet, before the night has come, have I lived to see the last warrior of the wise race of the Mohicans
— James Fenimore Cooper

Curve Lake, Ontario — Every man of fighting age in this Ojibwa reserve volunteered for the Second World War.

Every single one. Fifty men.

Actually, 51. But Cliff Whetung was allergic to the dyed wool of army uniforms. Swelled up like a balloon. So his war ended after a week, in a Peterborough hospital.

The last of the 50 is Cliff's kid brother Murray, 85 and sharp as a hunting knife.

"Must be the whisky," he tells me, eyes twinkling like the dark, shallow waters of Chemong Lake.

We are drinking green tea in his kitchen, deep in the woods. Oaks, maples, ash, in all the hues of autumn, sweep down to the shore.

It was called Mud Lake back then and 300 Ojibwa lived on a spit of nine square klicks, in the curve of adjoining lakes, minding their own business.

Murray Whetung hunted deer, fished walleye, trekked out to jobs in Peterborough, and wooed a beauty named Elva.

But not even Curve Lake was safe from the Nazis.

So the men enlisted. Five women, too. Whole families. The names in grey granite at the village cenotaph include 19

Mike Strobel/SUN MEDIA.

Every man at Curve Lake Ojibwa reserve, including Murray Whetung, signed up for World War II.

Taylors, five Knotts, three Irons, three Whetungs.

That's just the Second World War. In the First World War, all 20 young men of the reserve went over. Two of them went on to re-up, in their 40s, to fight Hitler.

So, 100 percent turnout in two wars. Still think Native Canadians aren't too committed to this country? From across Canada, 12,000 Natives fought. More than 500 were killed in the war, including two of Murray's childhood friends.

Muriland Knott, 15, lied about his age to sign up. He died last summer, Murray tells me, pointing to a white frame house a hop, skip from the cenotaph.

Tommy Prince, a Manitoba Ojibwa, joined the Devil's Brigade and won the Military Medal and the U.S. Silver Star.

Signalman Murray Whetung landed on Juno Beach, D-Day plus three. The Allies often used Native soldiers as snipers or scouts. "Code talkers," mostly Cree, befuddled Nazi spies. Murray strung telephone lines. Juno Beach to Germany.

A crack shot, he never had to use his Sten gun in anger. But he dodged German patrols and artillery trying to blow up his lines. He spent taut nights splicing cable at the front.

You get a good view of a war from atop a telephone pole and Murray Whetung saw things he'd rather he hadn't.

Six months after Germany surrendered, he came home. At the foot of Curve Lake Road, he met reserve men heading out to hunt.

"Leave me a canoe," he said, and ran home to trade his army bags for a rifle. Next morning, he bagged three deer.

Life goes on. Murray, who became a United Church minister, is the last of those 50 warriors. (A female veteran who married into the reserve after the war also survives.)

Last year, Murray declined an invite to the Juno Beach Centre's "Voices of the First Peoples of Canada" exhibit.

One tour of Europe was enough, he tells me.

Lung disease took Elva a decade ago. They had 13 kids. Curve Lake swarms with their great-grandkids. Would they all sign up to fight the Third World War, God forbid?

And why is so little known, by the rest of us, about what their kin did for king and country?

"First Nations traditions are oral," former chief Gary Williams, 47, tells me at the band office. "We've never written down our history."

So the rest of the country doesn't hear about mass volunteering or that most bands also sent money to the war effort. Maybe it was the tradition of alliance with Britain dating to the American Revolution. Maybe it was loyalty to Canada, despite everything.

Maybe it was the lure of adventure and paycheques when reserves were at their hard-bitten worst.

Doesn't matter. Our thanks is overdue.

Sunday at the cenotaph, the Maple Leaf will fly with the Union Jack and Curve Lake's banner, an eagle bearing a peace pipe.

Chief Keith Knott will speak. Everyone will sing "O Canada." Kids will read "In Flanders Fields." The Wshkiigomaang Women Hand Drum Singers will play as Murray Whetung, last of 50 brave men, lays a wreath.

The sun, if it is out, will gleam off the buckskin suit he and Elva stitched 40 years ago. For years, native garb was barred at any Remembrance Day ceremony. That was a shame.

Those medals sure look good on buckskin.

Now His Pal's His Hero, Too
(February 17, 2003)

Oh, I won't be afraid,
Just as long as you stand, stand by me
— "Stand by Me" by Ben E. King

Little Christopher goes under a second time. The dark waters of the Humber close over his head.

His snowboots touch the riverbed and he pushes with all the might a six-year-old can muster. The top of his aqua snowsuit breaks the surface, flashing in the brittle afternoon sun.

"Help, Michael, help!" he splutter-screams. And through the steam of his breath, he sees Michael scrambling toward him over the milky ice ...

— — —

It is Michael Murphy's 13th birthday.

As always, he watches Saturday morning cartoons. *Ninja Turtles* and *Ultra Man*.

The gang knocks on his apartment door and soon they are swarming over the toboggan hill. It slopes into the valley behind their low-rise apartment block on Weston Road south of Finch. It ends at a no-name creek that drains into the Humber, a 15-minute walk downstream.

The kids have Crazy Carpets and a Zellers push-cart to swoosh down the 45-degree hill. But mostly they body surf, over ground made slick by a thaw a week earlier.

Christopher Saulnier-Walton is the smallest, Michael the oldest. There's Christopher's brother Jordon, 10, Ariel Breedon, 12, and her brother Adrian, 11.

Michael's best pal Isaiah Cobb, 10, watches from his fourth-floor bedroom window. He's grounded for sassing a teacher.

Wind nears 40 clicks through the broad valley. It's, oh, -10.

They soon tire of pounding down the icy hill.

No one says, "Let's go." They simply strike off into the valley in the intuitive way of kids who've hung together, like always. Who've played "king of the hill" and pretended to be *Resident Evil* zombies skulking in the trees. Who name themselves after *Beyblades* characters. Kai. Tyson. Max.

Ariel, dark-haired and serious, leads most of them across the no-name creek, onto the flood plain of the Humber. There are tracks everywhere. Mice. Rabbits. The kids follow deer prints through the milkweed husks and burdock.

They give wide berth to a huge, gnarly locust tree hulking near where the creek trickles into the Humber. Under that tree is the home of The Bum, a shelter of sticks and tarp half dug into the ground.

The Bum once scared the bejeezus out of Ariel, rising from his lair, ranting about protecting yourself from the evil sun.

Someone heard he had moved on. But you can never be sure.

Michael and Christopher stay on No-name Creek's eastern banks, poking among the scrub maples. Hydro lines hum above them. A Rottweiler bays from a duplex way up on the valley's eastern flank. Somewhere a crow caws in protest.

Sound carries forever when it's cold and you're a kid. We've all been there, one time or another.

Christopher reaches the Humber first. He sees the rusty front wheel of a bicycle poke through near the bank. He wanders onto the ice, 15 metres to the middle of the river. He is five days from his seventh birthday.

Back among the maples, Michael hears the crack, the splash. He scurries down the bank, across the ice.

Christopher is scared to death, his face red as an apple. He sinks again. Rises again, spluttering, clinging to the ice's crumbly edge. The current tugs toward rapids downstream.

Michael crawls forward. Reaches, reaches ...

In he goes. Up to his neck. Shocked.

"I couldn't feel a thing," he will tell me later. "But I'm a Newfie and we're good with water. I wasn't even thinking. Christopher was screaming and I kept telling him, 'Calm down, we're gonna get out.'"

On his third try, he hoists his small friend onto solid ice.

Michael is spent, frozen, bruised by the ice. Feebly, he swings a leg out of the water, then starts to slide back in.

But Christopher grabs his coat sleeve. Their eyes meet. With a heave, Michael is out. They haul each other up the bank.

The splashes have brought the others running. Jordon gives his brother his balaclava. They all dash for home. It is 2:30 p.m., 13 years to the minute that Michael was born, a five-pound, 12-ounce preemie.

Grown-ups take over. Christopher goes to hospital. Any longer in that water, the doc tells Ken Walton, 33, and your son wouldn't be here. Michael sees his doctor. Both kids have hacking coughs most of last week.

Ken thinks: Michael saved my son and we should tell someone. So he calls us. Which brings me to the Humber with the kids, to hear what happened two Saturdays ago.

"Michael saved me," Christopher says. "He's my hero."

When he thaws out, Michael helps his mom, Isabella, 36, ice his birthday cake.

I'll bet double-fudge chocolate never tasted so good.

Could You Cut Off Your Own Arm?
(September 16, 2004)

"I would rather die of thirst than drink from the cup of mediocrity"
> — sign outside the Bank Note pub

Aron Ralston idly turns a steak knife in his left hand. Out a window of the Bank Note, Bathurst Street and everyday life hurry by.

Behind those green eyes, I think, he is back in that canyon in Utah.

"Do I wish I'd had a sharp knife like this?" he says when I ask. "I mean, I could have cut through it easy and been out of there sooner. But, no, no. I wouldn't change a thing."

Nothing? Not the pain? The grim, cold nights? The thirst? That decision?

"No. It was the greatest thing that's ever happened to me." The green eyes do not waver. They have seen things ...

— — —

May 1, 2003. Aron Ralston, 27, is trying to figure how to hack off his right forearm. His hand had been trapped between an 800-pound boulder and the canyon wall for six days.

He is a skilled climber and outdoorsman, but he is a long way from nowhere and no one knows where he is.

His water gone, he is left with his urine, his trances, Captain Kirk, family, and friends. He says farewells on his camcorder. A raven visits daily. A kangaroo rat nests nearby.

Oh, and Aron has one of those multi-tools, with two pullout pocket knives, a small file and pliers. One knife is ruined from chipping at the boulder, about the size of a bus tire.

That damn rock sat still maybe a million years. But it rolled as Aron climbed over and it caught him. It killed his hand in six hours. Cut off blood flow. Aron knew it early on.

"You're gonna have to cut your arm off," he told himself the first day. Later he tried the other knife, but the bone stopped him. The hand is numb. The wrist is agony.

Six days in, the hand is decomposing.

Aron Ralston waits to die. He has a vision. A blond boy. His son-to-be? A reason to live? An epiphany comes. Break the bone, Aron! Twist your arm, break it, then cut through with the knife!

What happens next is not for the weak of stomach. It takes him an hour. First, two ungodly snaps, like cap guns.

A tourniquet, then "sort, pinch, rotate, slice," he calls it. Skin and bone hurt like hell. Muscle doesn't. Nor tendon. He crunches through that with the pliers. The main nerve is murder.

Jeezuz, Aron.

"No, no. I was euphoric," he tells me. "I wanted rid of that hand. I think I had a huge shit-eating grin on my face.

"The pain was ... significant," he adds drily. "But you have to put it into the context of fighting for my life."

One last slash at skin and: "*I'm free!*"

But not out of the woods. He heads for his truck, eight miles away. He has to rappel down a cliff. One-handed. Incredible. At last, he runs into a Dutch family. Soon he is on a helicopter ride to hospital and recovery and home in Aspen, Colorado.

It is one helluva story. I cannot do it justice here.

Aron has put it in one helluva book. *Between a Rock and a Hard Place.*

At the Bank Note, he gets a cell call from New York. He has debuted at Number 8 on the Times' best-sellers list. He hoists a margarita in celebration. For six days last year, he dreamed of margaritas.

On his right arm, a steel claw. He has seven others, for different tasks. Guitar pickin'. Mountain climbing.

He misses clapping at rock concerts. "But, hey, I'm at a rock concert. I'm alive."

"You don't regret hiking into that canyon?"

"I wouldn't take my hand back. It's such a small trade-off for the sense of giving something positive to the world, showing people they can dig deeper, do more things than they think they can."

So he learned to write left-handed and gives talks. There is, as yet, no son-to-be, that "little boy who gave me the strength to know there was a future outside the canyon."

His sense of humour is whole. The last chapter is "A Farewell to Arm."

"Got another book in you?"

"Well, I hope it's not *How I Lost My Other Arm.*"

He chuckles and heads out, into the blur of everyday life. Everyday tasks. Everyday decisions.

DEAR MIKEY

I Want to Be an Advice Columnist. What Should I Do?
(March 8, 2009)

Sun Media is searching for an advice columnist.

The blurb says "we need someone with common sense and uncommon wit who has the answers to life's big questions. From family feuding to love and heartbreak to etiquette and child rearing, you'll have the final say."

I don't know why they're bothering to look outside the building for this all-knowing agony aunt. I've got some spare time and I'm constantly asked for advice ...

Dear Mikey:
My girlfriend won't let me out of bed. She is a wanton beast, I swear to God. Her idea of sex is anything goes, anywhere, anyhow, every hour on the hour. I'm losing weight, my eyes are baggy, I can't find any of my underwear and I'm neglecting work, friends, and family. My mom just had me declared legally dead. Help!
WHACKED OUT, WHITBY.
Dear WOW:
Quit whining and count your lucky stars, you wuss. You could be this next guy ...

Dear Mikey:
We never have sex, my wife and I. It's not that we don't want to. We sure do. But we're both too shy to initiate. So every night we stare awkwardly at each other, then fall into fitfull sleep. It's been 10 years and we're climbing the walls. How do we break the ice, open the floodgates and burst the dam?
RANDY IN RIVERDALE.
Dear Randy:
Piece of cake. You need a kickstart. Take a page from Ivan Pavlov, the Russian who trained dogs to salivate when they heard a bell. Start with verbal cues. Pick a word or

phrase that triggers sexual action in both of you.

From the sound of things, "Hello," ought to do it. I would avoid "the" or "and," lest you become like poor Whacked Out. Next, try audible cues. Bells and whistles, à la Pavlov, that make you salivate, so to speak. Or police sirens, though employ with caution in Scarborough or Rexdale.

Dear Mikey:

My boss at the bank is on my case again. This time it's not about my skills, punctuality, or work ethic, none of which, to be frank, are all that great. Now he's miffed because I wear torn jeans and a tank top every day.

Good grief, if he paid me better maybe I could afford snazzier clothes. Should I tell him to take his pinstripes and stuff 'em? SLOPPY SUE AT ST. CLAIR AND YONGE.

Dear Slob, I mean Sloppy:

My legal adviser tells me you have two options. Go topless, which is allowed in Toronto. If your boss objects, sue his chauvinistic ass. I can't tell from your letter if you're a teller at the bank. If so, perhaps you can suggest serving customers in similar attire. A slobs-only line. If nothing else, you'll meet a lot of panhandlers coming in to deposit the day's take.

Dear Mikey:
My teenage son got a nipple ring without telling me. I found out when it set off the security buzzer at Pearson. They made him take off his shirt. All the other moms looked at me like I was a dope. I'm so upset, I'm starting to rub off the ankle tattoo I got at a rave in 1994. What's with kids these days?
MOM'S THE WORD.
Dear MTW:
Rip it out when he's asleep. That'll teach him. And be happy he didn't get one of those trendy penile tattoos that sometimes say "Swan" and sometimes say "Saskatchewan."

Dear Mikey:
Hey, fella, I thought all advice columnists were women. You think you have the same sensitivity as a broad? C'mon. That picture of you in the paper dressed as a dame hardly qualifies. Unless the question is from a transvestite.
SKEPTICAL IN SCARBOROUGH.
Dear SINS:
Get off your fat gender bias. Who says men can't be wise and motherly? Look at Robin Williams in Mrs. Doubtfire or Dustin Hoffman in Tootsie. Rest assured I shall dispense my advice while wearing a shawl and smelling of fresh baked bread.

You see? Perfect. I'll be Sun Media's agony uncle. "Dear Abby," eat your heart out.

How to Behave on a Nude Beach
(January 7, 2009)

RUNAWAY BAY, Jamaica — "So, you work for the *Sun*," says a Toronto man with an all-over tan.

How on earth could you tell?

"I saw your ass."

Oh, jeez. The tattoo. A *Sun* logo has blazed from my right cheek since a moment of silliness a few years back. Usually, except for momentary frights in the bathroom mirror, it's easy to forget.

Not on a nude beach.

"And I see you work for Volkswagen," I tell the all-over tan man.

His brow wrinkles, like most of the rest of him.

"Oh, that," he says. "That's just a mole." And he jiggles back into the sea.

So join me, at least in spirit, on the nude beach at beautiful but cruelly named Pear Tree Bottom. It basks on sweeping Runaway Bay on the north shore of this twinkling isle.

It is a modest nude beach, pardon the expression. No Vera Playa or Haulover. No Little Banana Beach (named by the Greeks for its curving yellow sand, silly). No Wreck Beach or even Hanlan's Point.

And certainly not the sex-soaked sands of Hedonism III across Runaway Bay.

Pear Tree Bottom's nude beach might hold 100 people tops, cheek by jowl. But the view is stunning. Out to sea, I mean. The reef bustles with barracuda, rays, lobster, and fish of every hue.

The beach teems with Canadians mostly. You can tell them by the frost-bitten nipples. They are not easy to interview, since I have nowhere to keep my tape recorder.

"We all have the same equipment," Mike Beniusis, 49, a Montreal teacher, reassures me.

Speak for yourself, pal. My tape recorder has two speeds.

Mike is a nude beach veteran. He has come to Pear Tree Bottom with the fetching Guylaine Roussel, 33. At least, I assume she's fetching. Her eyes are fetching. I stare resolutely into them.

See, nude beaches have rules. Not leering is one. Maintain eye contact. "*Dans les blanc des yeux*," says Guylaine. The whites of the eyes.

Or gaze at the sky. Do NOT stare directly at the sun. You will go blind, and your palms will get hairy.

I know these things. Learned them the hard way, beginning long ago at Wreck Beach when I had a physique worth leering at.

Other tips:

1. If you are a single man wearing dark glasses and lurking in the shade, you are suspect.

    "*Sceneux*," says Guylaine. Peeping Tom. The Germans have a special word for you: *Freikorperkultur-pervertieren*. If you're creepy enough, the skinny-dippers will call the cops or oust you. And you don't want naked men swarming you like locusts.
2. Know the difference between "nude beach" and "clothing optional". The latter is mixed company. At a real nude beach, such as Pear Tree Bottom, you have to take it all off.
3. Bring a towel, though, especially if there's a beach bar. I mean, who needs you flopping your sandy butt all over the bar stool. Gross.
4. Which brings us to an eternal male debate on a nude beach. Is it bad form to become, you know, scintillated? Or is it worse to not? Men are troubled

by such questions. Ask any woman. Some of us never find an answer. We just stick our heads in the sand.

5. Sunscreen. Need I say more? But do not ask the cute girl under the next palm umbrella to apply it to your hard-to-reach places. That puts you in a special category of *Freikorperkultur-pervertieren*.

6. Swim with caution. Coral reef can sting. Not to mention, fellas, you're packing your own built-in live bait. What if a near-sighted barracuda swims by?

Or even a hungry minnow.

From One Fatty to Another
(February 15, 2009)

Poor Jessica Simpson. Everyone's picking on her for getting porky.

US Weekly: "Jessica's Agony! Bullied for her weight! How she's tortured by food!"

The New York Post: "Jumbo Jessica!"

In Touch: "I'm Not Fat!"

People: "Stop Calling Her Fat!"

Jessica even bumped Barack Obama and his family off the cover of the latest *US*. The skinny new president then quipped about the singer's "weight battle."

Jessica is devastated by the catty onslaught. A friend tells *In Touch*: "She has been crying a lot."

I know how she feels. Two months ago I topped 231 pounds, a.k.a. 105 kilos.

Oh, the humiliation! My boobs jiggled. Nothing fit. Store clerks winked when I asked for XXL. Children ran for their lives when I jumped in the pool.

My own mother called me "Lard-Ass."

But no more. As I write this, I weigh a nifty 198.

"How'd you do it!?" asked an envious colleague. "You should tell people."

So I will. I hope Jessica Simpson reads this.

I'm not saying fat can't be beautiful. It can. Just not on me. So here's how I lost 33 pounds in two months. I call it the "Scarberia Diet." (Disclaimer: Mike Strobel is not a doctor. He does not even have basic first aid. Use his diet advice at your own risk and with a grain of salt. The *Sun* bears no responsibility.)

First, get really, really fat. No fun losing weight if you're three pounds over ideal. The before and after photos will be meaningless.

Me, I ballooned to 29 pounds heavier than 202, the upper limit of normal for my six foot one. I achieved this with a cocktail of beer, wine, TV, late-night snacks, and more beer and wine.

Next, when you are really rolly-polly, have a health scare. A heart attack, say. Or getting stuck in a phone booth. In my case, the extra girth plus some cold remedies spiked my blood pressure.

Dr. Sherryn Roth, a cardiologist at Scarborough General, looked at me with pity and said, "You gained 30 pounds and your blood pressure went up? Go figure."

"You mean I'm not gonna die?"

"We all die sooner or later."

The way she said it chilled me to the bone. Even through all my blubber. So I vowed to get trim.

I cut out all booze. ALL booze. The shock alone will knock 10 pounds out of you. No coffee either. I think 20 or 30 cups a day was making me retain water.

Moderation? Never works. It's for suckers. All or nothing — and it's nothing if you want to lose weight.

For breakfast, have some sort of powder. Do NOT use powder that must be snorted or smoked. Sure, you will lose weight, but the side effects are a killer. I drink whey protein powder. It tastes like sand, which puts me off food until noon.

For lunch, a skinless barbecued chicken breast and salad. Every day. No silly mulling over menus.

Avoid salt like Lot's wife. Not only table salt. Some processed foods are mini salt mines. Bad for your blood pressure. Plus you retain water.

If the package says "210% of daily sodium requirement," skip it.

Forget about dinner. Forever.

If that's too drastic, don't eat anything after 8 p.m. It sticks to your midriff like cold porridge.

Get off your lard ass. Walk, then run. Lift weights. But go *easy*. A wrecked Achilles tendon helped me get lazy and fat in the first place.

There's another thing. Blame something, or someone, for you being a pig. The misdirected anger burns 50 calories a day.

See how simple it is? Calories in, calories out.

One last thing. Try to ditch excess baggage in your life.

If Jessica Simpson could just lose 224 pounds of party-going quarterback, she'd be back in those Daisy Duke shorts in no time.

One Way to Whip This Crime Spree
(November 3, 2005)

Gang bullets buzz past an 8-year-old girl on Sackville Street at about the same time a letter arrives on my desk from a nice couple in Alliston.

The Osmonds are in their 80s.

"Since no one seems to have a solution for cutting down crime in Toronto," they write, "here's one thing that worked in the past."

They enclose an old newspaper clipping. It tells of how Winnipeg handled a crime wave a century ago.

"We had a series of highway robberies," the police chief told the newspaper. "The lash ended them."

One hood got 75 strokes, another got 50. Winnipeg had nary another highway robbery for 15 years.

In the Big Smoke these days, it is hard to imagine a 15-hour pause in gang gunplay, let alone 15 years.

Now, before you say, "Mike, you're nuts. We can't just start flogging people," consider a few things.

Mainly, jail sentences and probation just aren't cutting it. The creeps are laughing at us. There's a clear need for something else. Why not corporal punishment? A well-aimed lash or two.

Consider, also, input from far greater minds than mine.

Dr. Graeme Newman is Distinguished Teaching Professor of Criminal Justice at the State University of New York at Albany. Brainy enough for you?

Professor Newman has authored several books, the bestselling being *Just and Painful: A Case for the Corporal Punishment of Criminals.* "Chapter 14, A Punishment Manifesto," suggests electric shock for most property crimes because "it can be scientifically controlled and calibrated."

Violent criminals, it says, who terrify or humiliate their victims should get a dose of their own medicine: a good whipping.

And no monkeying about. The first lash should fall before the echo of "guilty" dies out.

"This is the most humane and just way to match the punishment to the crime," the good professor tells me down the line from upstate New York. "We need something, between the extremes of prison and probation, that is credible to the public."

Not like the case I wrote about last week. A guy who gored a housemate with a steak knife was sentenced to two years of 8 p.m. curfew at his parents' place.

Would fear of the lash keep Toronto's new gangs from ventilating each other and sometimes innocent bystanders?

"I doubt it," says Newman. "They're so used to violence." Giving and receiving it is almost a badge.

So corporal punishment is less a deterrent and more a quicker, more visible, satisfying, cheaper option to long prison terms. You solve gang violence by getting to its root, such as giving poor kids better options, says the professor.

True, but I still think your average Toronto gangster would think twice about pulling his 9mm if he knew a lashing was the price.

But, Mike, we haven't flogged folks since the 1870s. Not in Canada. At least none that didn't want it.

Try the 1970s. Yep, lashing was law until 1972, the year we beat Russia in the big series, and was used nearly to the end.

Canada's prison museum curator David St. Onge tells me 333 cons took a licking between 1957 and 1968, the year of an inquiry into the practice. The peak was 1963, with 96.

Swear at a guard? Try to escape? You faced, so to speak, a leather paddle while reclining on a "punishment bench."

Cat-o'-nine-tails was the choice for court sentences.

Rape, indecent assault, incest, drugging, and armed robbery could get you the whip, a sawed-off broom handle and nine strands like curtain cord with knots at each end.

In 1970, a Hamilton hood got eight years and 10 lashes for beating an old man and robbing him of 85 bucks.

Quirky thing about those lashes. You got half on arrival at prison and the rest when you left. ("Good news is you're out next week. Bad news is ...")

Usually 10 prison staff saw the show, including a doctor.

St. Onge says ex-cons turn up at his Kingston museum. They bring their grandkids, regale them with tales of the lash.

I bet none of those grandkids join gangs.

Reunion? Stay Sober and Know Who's Dead
(October 1, 2005)

Time travel can get bumpy.

A barfly I barely knew 32 years ago corners me.

"Mike Strooooobel?!"

"'Fraid so."

"I remember you. You were scrawny. ScrAWWWny. I used to think, 'ewwww, Mike Strooooobel ...'" and she pretends to gag.

"Yes, well, I was quite slend —"

"Lookit you now. You're much ... thicker."

Yeoww. High School Reunion. Enter At Own Risk.

First question. How the devil did Barfly get so jolly?

True, the Class of '73, Uxbridge Secondary School, was very merry in its heyday. Ask anyone who lived within a bottle-toss of Siloam Hall on a Friday night.

But this reunion is dry. "We still don't drink," warns the invite from Don the Baptist. He wed a belle of our class, Fay Morris.

Don and I used to have great theological debates after basketball practice. Don feared I was bound for hell if I did not mend my ways, and he was nearly right. The newspaper racket may not be hell, but it's in the neighbourhood.

I should have listened, too, when Don said the Lord will provide.

This dawns on me as night falls and we pull up to his gate south of Uxbridge. It is soaring iron and an intercom. Beyond are 20 hectares of trees, trails, and ponds, and a looming mountain of a house. Five storeys. An elevator.

Don helped build a little outfit called Clearnet. Telus bought it for 6.6 billion bucks.

Should have stuck closer to that boy.

But no time for regrets. The reunion awaits. It is in honour of us turning 50.

Part of a columnist's job is to experience things for you. So you can navigate life's curves. Thus some handy hints to survive, even enjoy, your high school reunion:

Have an opening line. Practise it. Something witty, but heartfelt. Do not, as I did, walk into the big room and blurt out, "Wow, look at all the old farts."

Wear name tags. Tacky, maybe, but after 32 years identities, even genders, blur. You do not want to say, "Hullo, Biff," to someone named Barbie.

And **don't sneak up behind people**. Approach from the front, chest out, so they can see your name.

Booze and memories do not mix. Stay sober. You need your wits about you.

And **steer clear of the drunks**. Nothing will make you grey faster than listening to a slurry life story.

Rent a Ferrari. A new one costs two grand a day, but you can rent a classic red 308 from Panache for $400.

Your schoolmates will think you changed your name to Tom Selleck. Or you can be like Mike Farlow, our class comedian. In '73 he drove a 1960 Vauxhall, puke green. Now he drives a 1961 Vauxhall, puke green.

Know who is dead and alive. Otherwise, if you say, "Sorry to hear about Bob," do not be surprised if Bob comes out of a shadow and says, "Whatcha mean?"

Sadly, our class has lost two mates, I just found out. The sweetest girl was killed in a car wreck. The sweetest guy, a model, died of liver failure.

The women look better than the men. Is this genetic? Biological? Environmental? Or is it just that the women who really went to seed are smart enough not to show up at the reunion?

We men have not noticed how we look, and don't care anyway.

The exception is always The Quarterback. Ours has hair as wavy, a jaw as chiselled, teeth as shiny as they ever were.

No comb-overs, please. I saw a poll that 99 percent of Canadian women loathe them. Bald is beautiful. Do not try to hide it with a rug. Especially if there are playful drunks.

Arrive late. It is harder to see your wrinkles in the dark.

And **relax**. Most important of all. Listen, why sweat it? You haven't seen these people in 32 years. You may not see them for another 32.

Maybe at your funeral. Then you won't have to worry about an opening line.

Kissing Lessons from the Professor
(February 4, 2009)

Valentine's Day draws near. Pucker up. Professor Strobel's kissing class is in session.

Yessiree, sweet lips, if there's one thing I know, it's kissing.

Don't ask me about all the messy stuff that comes after. But I have clinched in the catacombs of Rome, locked lips beneath the Eiffel Tower, pecked a dilly in Piccadilly, bussed in Central Park, and snogged in the Amazon jungle.

And not once have I drawn blood. So read and learn ...

A man's kiss is his signature, as much-kissed Mae West used to purr. And as we fellers know, the pressure to be a good kisser has never been higher.

Lips are in overdrive this century. We have not seen the likes since Clark Gable rammed his dentures into Vivien Leigh in *Gone with the Wind*.

Today, our ladies measure us against a legion of tonsil masseurs.

Viggo Mortensen, with Liv Tyler in *Return of the King*. Leonardo "Kiss Me Kate" DiCaprio on the prow of the Titanic. Ryan Gosling in the teeming rain with Rachel McAdams in *The Notebook*. Spider-Man upside down with Kirsten Dunst.

Even Madonna and Britney Spears on stage at an MTV awards show. How the hell can a guy compete with Madonna in the tonsil hockey game?

Well, that's where I come in. Let's start with the most common question: size. Novice kissers seeking my advice often ask, "But, what if my tongue isn't long enough?"

Relax, pal. It's all in your head. Women don't care.

Since when is the esophagus an erogenous zone? As long as you can play Chopsticks on her palate, she's happy.

But, hold on, buster, take a step back. Tongue is the last card you play in the kissing game. Start with ambiance and setting. The great kisses all do. Burt Lancaster and Deborah Kerr in *From Here To Eternity*, say.

Two lovers mesh on a Hawaii beach, the frothy Pacific lapping at their loins. Burt could be kissing a sea turtle and it would look hot.

Since Hawaii is an expensive trip, for just a kiss, a simple adjustment of lighting will do for mood. At least then she can't see your nose hairs.

"But, Professor, how do I even know she wants to be kissed?"

My friend, the worst thing you can do is ask her. She doesn't want to kiss a wimp. Rhett didn't ask Scarlett. He just knew.

How? If you're lucky, she takes the guesswork out and growls, "Kiss me, you fool." In my experience, that rarely happens, except the "you fool" part.

So, watch her body language. It's a good sign if she licks her lips. Or closes her eyes and opens her mouth. (Careful, she might just be about to sneeze!)

Also, I advise against kissing a girl if you do not know her name. Or at least her stage name.

I recommend a light brush on the cheek first. (Not that cheek, silly. The one next to her nose.) If she slaps you just for that, your night is toast. But if she holds still and sighs, turn your lips to starboard.

Go slow! Nothing kills the mood like a chipped tooth. Dentists get rich on first kisses. Light touches to start. The lips are loaded with nerve endings.

No drooling. No swishing, swirling or sucking. She's not a Slurpee, for crying out loud.

It is okay to moisten your lips first, to avoid chaffing.

Do *not* burp. (And surely I need not mention freshen your breath and brush your tongue.)

Listen with your lips. How is she responding? If she has bitten off your tongue, or she is dialling 911 on her cellphone, then you're overdoing it. If she says she wants to have your baby, all's well.

So far so good?

Now, when to break it off. Sadly, there is no such thing as a neverending kiss. Unless you both wear braces.

Again, read her mood. If she's snoring, disengage. If she's still babbling about that baby, then move on to the next step. But you're on your own. We're a family newspaper.

You have 10 days to practise kissing before February 14. Tape this column to the fridge for reference.

I hope I haven't been too tongue in cheek.

ABOUT THE AUTHOR

Mike Strobel is a columnist for the *Toronto Sun,* and a veteran newspaper writer and editor. But the loftiest gig of his press career may have been his first: paper boy for Parliament Hill, a job that paid for a near-degree in journalism from Carleton University.

Born on a tobacco farm near Tillsonburg, Ontario, Strobel has lived mostly in the east end of Toronto, especially Scarborough. You need a rugged sense of humour to survive in that suburb, which is why comic actor Mike "Austin

Powers" Myers, for instance, is the way he is.

Strobel has since fled downtown, fending off panhandlers, hipsters, and poodles in designer sweaters. This has not slowed his output of four or five columns a week in the up-front news pages of the *Sun*, efforts that have won a dozen newspaper awards and millions of hits on *torontosun.com*.

Strobel's columns are an offbeat look at life on the streets and in the living rooms of Toronto and beyond. Mostly they make you laugh, but sometimes they make you rage, and sometimes they make you cry. They offer skewed wisdom on the likes of love, weight loss, and, ahem, male enhancement. They cover City Hall, Hollywood and hockey, scammers, panhandlers, and swingers.

In the 1980s and 1990s, after starting at the *Ottawa Journal*, Strobel was managing editor of the *Calgary Sun* and editor-in-chief of the *Toronto Sun*, before coming to his senses and returning to writing in 2001.

MORE GREAT HUMOUR FROM DUNDURN

Script Tease
by Eric Nicol
978-1-55488-707-1
$19.99

Why write in the first place, other than your grocery list? Eric Nicol believes it's the second-most satisfying thing you can do lying down. But it's not enough to want to write. You must *need* to write. Now, after more than seventy years of scribbling Nicol holds forth on dangling participles, punctuation, and literary jargon. What's more, he answers the burning question: "How much should creative writers depend on editors to correct their grammar?" Then Eric provides a wide selection of essays to demonstrate how it's done. Pure Nicol. Minted in Canada. Priceless!

Old Is In
by Eric Nicol
978-1-55002-524-8
$16.99

Is impotence contagious? At what age should a senior be surgically separated from his automobile, or obligated to donate his sex toys to the Salvation Army? These and other timely questions are among those not answered in Eric Nicol's latest cure for serious reading. This palsied opus responds to demographics warning that our Western society is about to be engulfed by a tidal wave of seniors. How to cope? Is stoicism the answer? Hell, no! The best way to relieve the stiff upper lip is with a smile. And that prescription is filled, merrily, by Eric Nicol's *Old Is In*.

DUNDURN PRESS
www.dundurn.com

What did you think of this book?
Visit www.dundurn.com
for reviews, videos, updates, and more!